Get ready for... Flyers

2nd Edition

OXFORD

UNIVERSITY PRESS

Hello!

Words

1 **Listen and read.** 🔊1

Holly   Harry

Holly: Hello! Our names are Holly and Harry Brown. We're ten years old.

Harry: We're twins. We drew our family tree.

2 **Look and answer the questions. Then complete Holly's diary.** P 128

1 What is Harry and Holly's surname?

2 How many grandchildren do the grandparents have?

3 Who is Harry's cousin?

4 How many brothers and sisters has Harry got?

5 Who is grown-up but not married?

6 Who is Holly's aunt?

3 **Draw your family tree and talk to your friends about it.**

Story

1 Listen and read. Then act. 🔊2

1 — The children are playing in the park.
I want to count!
OK, we're going to hide.
You count to a thousand.

2 — This way, Katy.
Come on, George.
One, two, three ...

3 — ... four hundred and thirty seven, eight hundred and eighty two, nine hundred and ninety nine ...

4 — ... a thousand. Coming, ready or not! I can see you!
You didn't count to a thousand!

2 Look at the story. Write the words for these numbers.

a 882 _____

b 1000 _____

3 Listen to the rhyme and number the months of the year. 🔊3

February ☐

October ☐

November ☐

April ☐

January 1

September ☐

December ☐

March ☐

May ☐

July ☐

August ☐

June ☐

1 Our home

Words

1 Complete the words for the things in Holly and Harry's home.

1 f r i d g e

2 c _ _ k _ r

3 b _ n

4 o _ _ n

5 r _ _ k _ _ k

6 s _ _ _ _ _

7 m _ _ _ r _ r

8 t _ _ _ p _ _ e

9 v _ _ l _ n

10 d _ u _ s

This is our home! Do you like it?

2 What are these things? Order the letters to find the words.

1
s p a o o h m

s h a m p o o

2
r h s u b

_ _ _ _ _ _

3
p e e o l v n e

_ _ _ _ _ _ _

4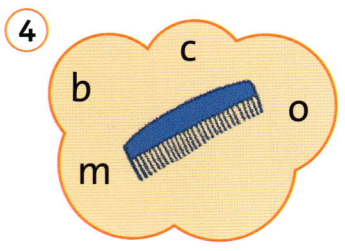
b c o m

_ _ _ _

5
p t s a s m

_ _ _ _ _ _

6
e r t l e t

_ _ _ _ _ _

7
s t p r o d c a

_ _ _ _ _ _ _

8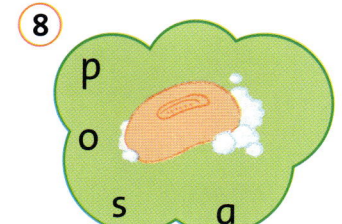
p o s a

_ _ _ _

9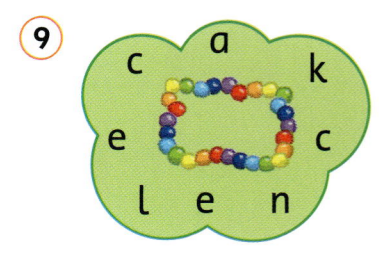
c a k e c l e n

_ _ _ _ _ _ _

Listening & speaking

1 Holly and Harry are getting ready for school. Where are their things? Listen and write the things under each place. 🔊 4

_____ _____ _____ _____

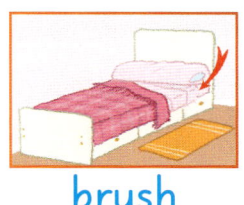

brush _____ _____ _____

2 Draw lines to match the words and pictures. Complete the sentences.

empty   broken   full   quiet   noisy   tidy   untidy

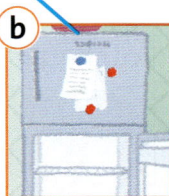
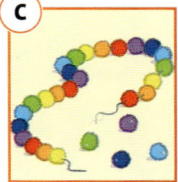

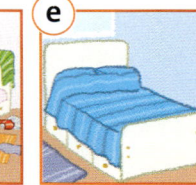

a   b   c   d   e   f   g

1 Harry's bedroom is very ___tidy___.

2 Look! Mum's necklace is _____.

3 The fridge was _____, so Dad went to the shop.

4 Holly's mum isn't happy because her bedroom is always so _____.

5 Be _____ please! Emma's sleeping.

6 I don't like going into Harry's room. He's always so _____!

7 I can't throw this paper in the bin because it's _____.

3 Do the speaking activity. **P** 129

Where's the soap?

It's on the shelf above the bed.

Story

1 **Listen and read. Then act.** 🔊 5

1 Where's Harry? **Someone**'s got my diary!

Everyone's in the living room.

2 I can't find my diary **anywhere**!

This is an important programme. Be quiet, please!

3 **No one**'s got your diary! I think it's in your bedroom **somewhere**.

4 There are clothes **everywhere**! Of course you can't find **anything**! Let's put **everything** away.

5 Look, here's your diary.

Thanks Mum!

6 I need to get **something** for dinner. Can **anyone** see my keys?

Oh Mum!

2 **Look at the words in orange in the story. Complete the sentences.**

Places	Things	People
There are clothes _everywhere_!	Let's put _____ away.	_____ is in the living room.
I think it's in your bedroom _____.	I need to get _____ for dinner.	_____ has got my diary!
I can't find my diary _____!	Of course you can't find _____!	Can _____ see my keys?
		_____ has got your diary.

Look! We use 'any' for questions and negatives.

GRAMMAR Pronouns with *every-, some-, no-* and *any*

Reading & writing

1 **Read and write the words in the gaps.**

① nothing   noisy   popular   bored   ~~everyone~~

"Harry's my brother and (**a**) _everyone_ says he looks like me. That's because we're twins! But he's different from me. He isn't quiet. He's very (**b**) _____! He plays his drums very loudly. At school, Harry's got lots of friends. He's really (**c**) _____ ! At the moment, Harry's (**d**) _____ because he says he's got (**e**) _____ to do."

② lucky   kind   untidy   everywhere   everything

"Everyone likes Holly because she's very (**a**) _____ . She plays games with our sister Emma and always chats to her. Holly's very (**b**) _____ . She leaves all her things (**c**) _____ ! But I think I'm (**d**) _____ because I've got a twin sister and she knows (**e**) _____ about me! It's fun!"

③ broken   unhappy   little   friendly   empty

"This is our (**a**) _____ sister, Emma. She's only three. We all love her because she's a nice, (**b**) _____ girl and she always plays with us. But she can be naughty. Sometimes she throws her toys everywhere and some of them get (**c**) _____ . She's (**d**) _____ at the moment. She's crying because her glass of milk is (**e**) _____ !"

④ anything   clever   unkind   boring   difficult

"This is our older brother, William. I think he's (**a**) _____ because he shouts at us! His teacher says he's very (**b**) _____ because he does well in tests. We think he's (**c**) _____ because he never does (**d**) _____ interesting. He always plays chess with his friend! He says he can't teach us because we're too young and it's a very (**e**) _____ game! And then he just says 'Go away!' to us."

Words

1 **Match to make words. Write the words.**

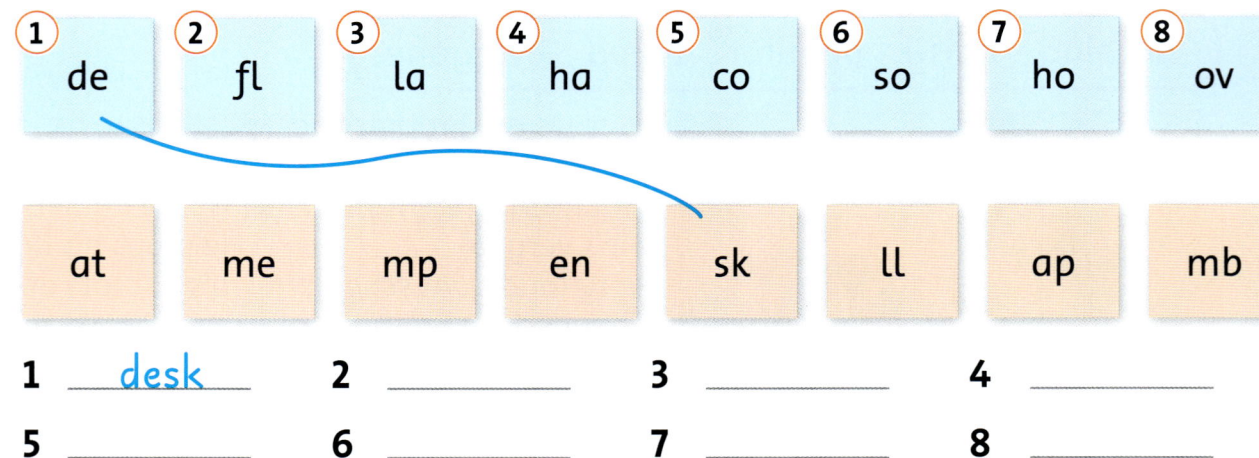

① de	② fl	③ la	④ ha	⑤ co	⑥ so	⑦ ho	⑧ ov

at	me	mp	en	sk	ll	ap	mb

1 ___desk___ 2 _____ 3 _____ 4 _____

5 _____ 6 _____ 7 _____ 8 _____

2 **Look at the pictures. Write the words in the word wheels.**

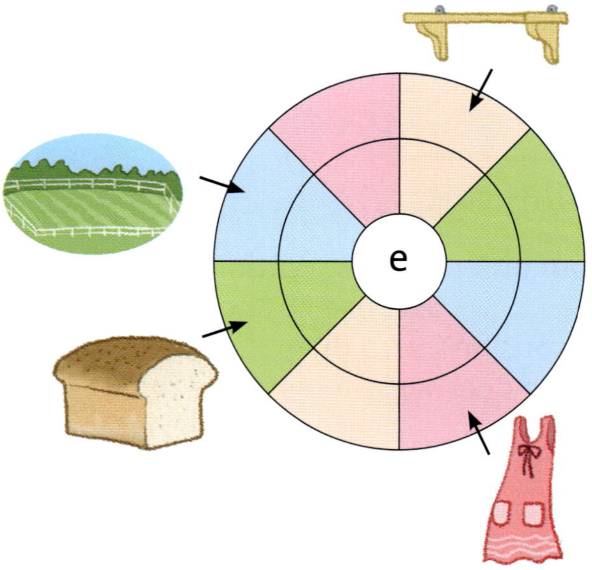

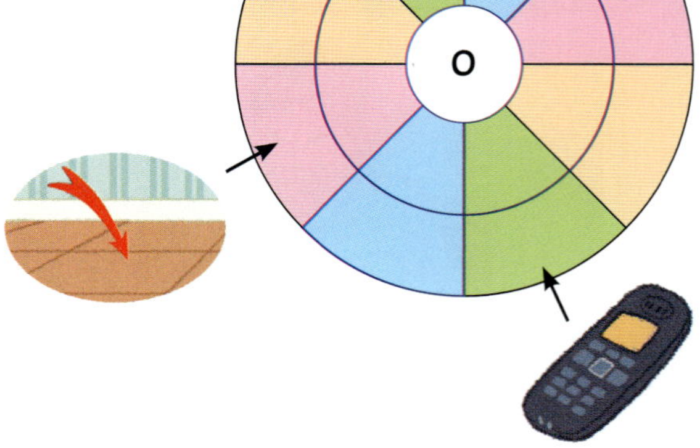

Word wheel: center **u** — h, o, r, s

Word wheel: center **a**

Word wheel: center **e**

Word wheel: center **o**

Extended reading: Holly's diary

1 Read Holly's diary. Order the pictures.

Read my diary!

2 Read the diary again and complete the text.

9th January

Dear Diary

Today was a not a good day! We (1) ____were____ late for school on our first day back after the holidays! Mum couldn't find her (2) _____ again! We looked for them (3) _____ and they were on the fridge all the time! Then Mum said Harry had (4) _____ comb his hair! We cycled to school but we arrived very late and the teacher was angry with us. Our teacher (5) _____ called Mr Pepper. I don't like him very much. He's always very unfriendly. After lunch I had my music lesson. My music teacher wasn't happy because I (6) _____ have my violin with me. I forgot to bring it to school so I had to borrow one. Then some of the children in our class (7) _____ very noisy in the classroom so our teacher gave us lots of homework. Now I can't (8) _____ out anywhere this weekend because of all my homework. I think our teacher was very unkind.

GRAMMAR *After* and *Before* clauses page 118

Flyers practice test

Look and read. Choose the correct words and write them on the lines. There is one example.

cushions   a bracelet   shorts   soap

pyjamas   files

an oven   a shelf

wifi   programmes

trainers   a fridge

You put things on this to keep your room tidy.   _a shelf_

1 This is like a necklace but it's smaller.   _____

2 You need this if you want to search for things on the internet.   _____

3 You find this in a bottle in the bathroom and use it when you wash your hair.   _____

4 This is part of a cooker. You put the food you want to cook in it.   _____

5 You find this in the bathroom. Water comes out of it and you go under it to get clean.   _____

6 You have these on sofas and armchairs. They're very nice to sit on.   _____

7 You put these on your feet when you want to run or play sport.   _____

8 You keep your work on the computer in these. You open them to find something and close them when you've finished.   _____

9 There are many different kinds of these on television. Some are about sport and others are about the news.   _____

10 People put these on when they go to bed at night.   _____

a shower   films   shampoo

Flyers practice test

Where are the things that David's mum needs for the trip?
Listen and write a letter in each box. There is one example. 🔊6

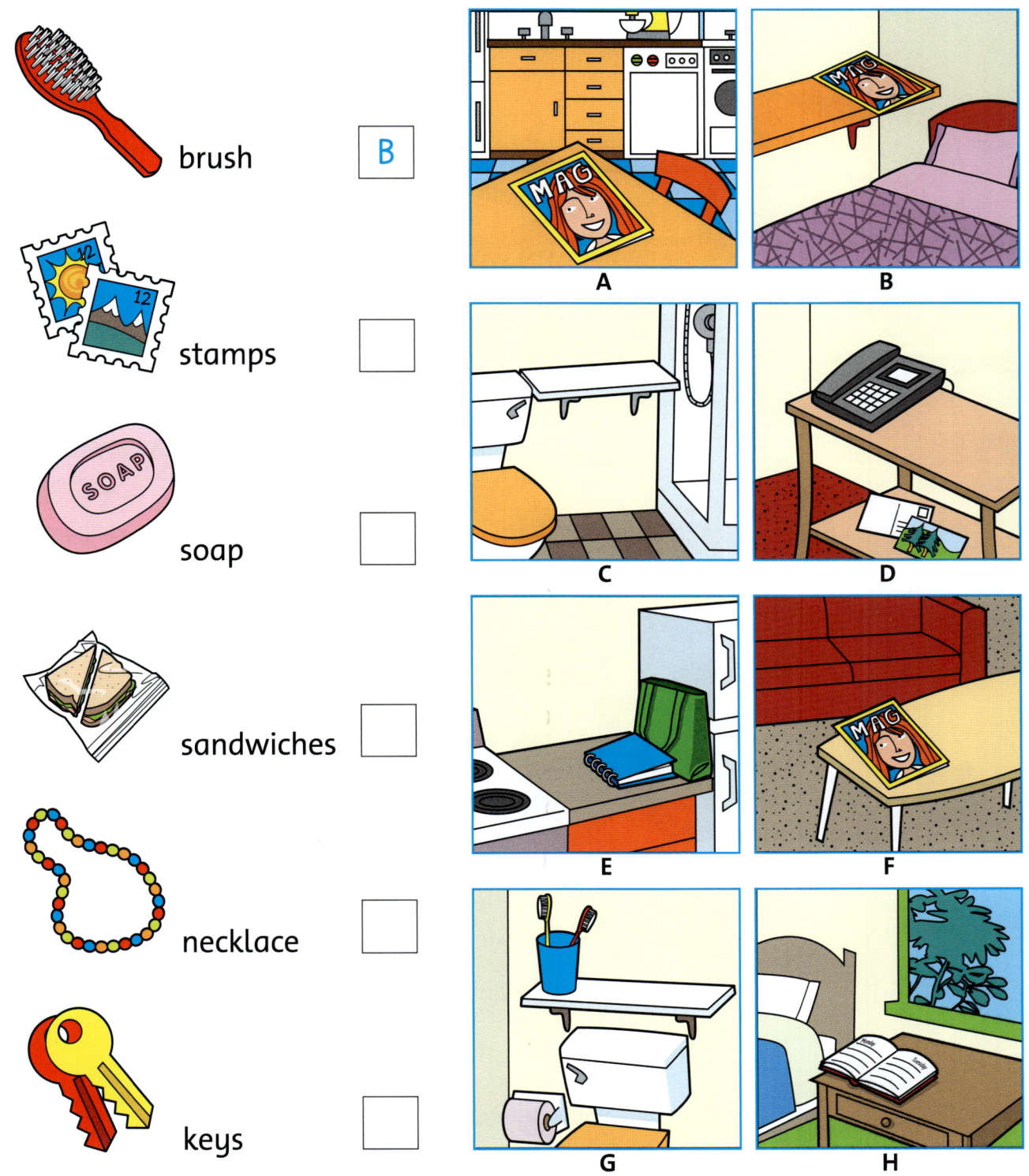

brush **B**

stamps

soap

sandwiches

necklace

keys

2 Going to town

Words

1 Find the places on the map and number the words.

Here's a map of the town where we live.

These are all the things you can find in the centre of our town!

university	10	hotel		chemist's	
airport		fire station		skyscrapers	
taxi		police station		sky	
traffic		railway station		stadium	
bicycles		motorway		post office	
ambulance		museum		hills	
fire engine		factory		bank	

Reading & speaking

1 Read. Look at the map on page 12 and write *yes* or *no*.

1 The chemist's is next to the bank.   _no_

2 There are some skyscrapers next to the hospital.   _____

3 The motorway is behind the hotel.   _____

4 The hotel is between the swimming pool and the airport.   _____

5 There's a bus stop round the corner from the house.   _____

6 From the factory, go straight on, past the cinema and you
   get to the university.   _____

7 There's a car park in front of the police station.   _____

8 The stadium is in front of the railway station.   _____

2 Do the speaking activity. P 130

From the restaurant go past the park and it's on the left.

You're at the fire station!

3 Where could Holly buy these things? Look at the map on page 12 and make suggestions.

Remember! We say 'She **buys**' but we say 'She could **buy**.'

GRAMMAR *could* page 118

Conversation

1 Listen and read. Then act. 🔊 7

Mum: Harry, fetch my glasses, please. I need to look at my shopping list.

Harry: Here they are, Mum.

Mum: William, will you go to town with Holly and Harry, please?

Holly: Yeah!

Mum: I need you to do lots of things! They're all here on the list.

William: Oh Mum!

Mum: And don't forget the money ... and my shopping list!

William: Oh, OK, Mum!

Mum: And will you change these shorts? I bought them for Harry but they're too small. Please don't forget!

William: OK Mum! See you later!

Who wants to go to town?

Who doesn't want to go to town?

2 Match the words with the pictures.

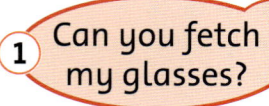
1 Can you fetch my glasses?

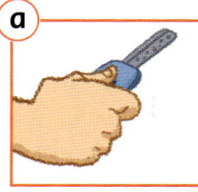 a

 b

4 Get off the bus at the supermarket.

2 Don't forget the key!

 c

 d

5 Could you post the letters, please?

3 Get on the bus at the bus stop round the corner.

 e

 f

6 Remember to change the shorts.

3 Ask and answer these questions with a friend.

How often / go / town?

How / travel / town?

Do / ever / go / bus?

What / buy?

What / your mum and dad / buy?

What / your favourite place / town?

Listening & speaking

1 Listen and number the places the children need to go. 🔊8

    1

2 Draw a map from your house to your school. Tell your friend about your map.

3 Holly is talking to her mum. What did the children do? What didn't they do? Listen and tick (✓) or cross (✗) the boxes. 🔊9

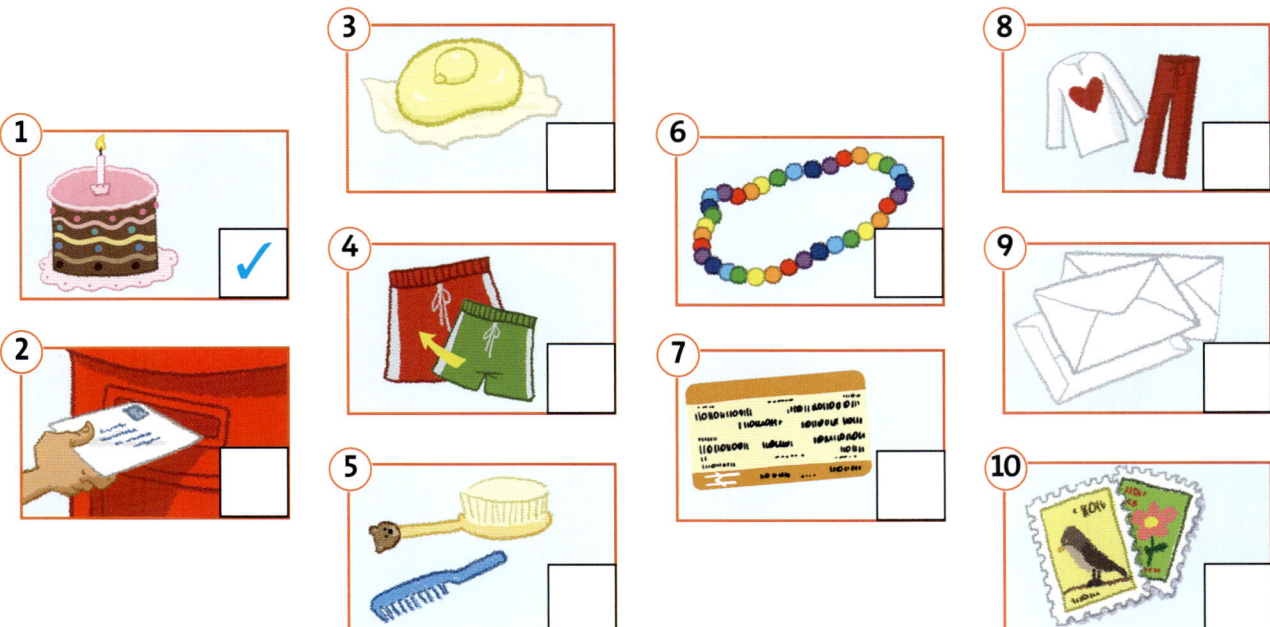

William bought something Mum didn't ask for. What was it?

A _____

Words

1 **Look at this picture. Find things beginning with the letter 's' and write a list.**

How many things did you find? _____

How long did it take you to find them? _____

2 **Write the words in the boxes and find the name of a shop.**

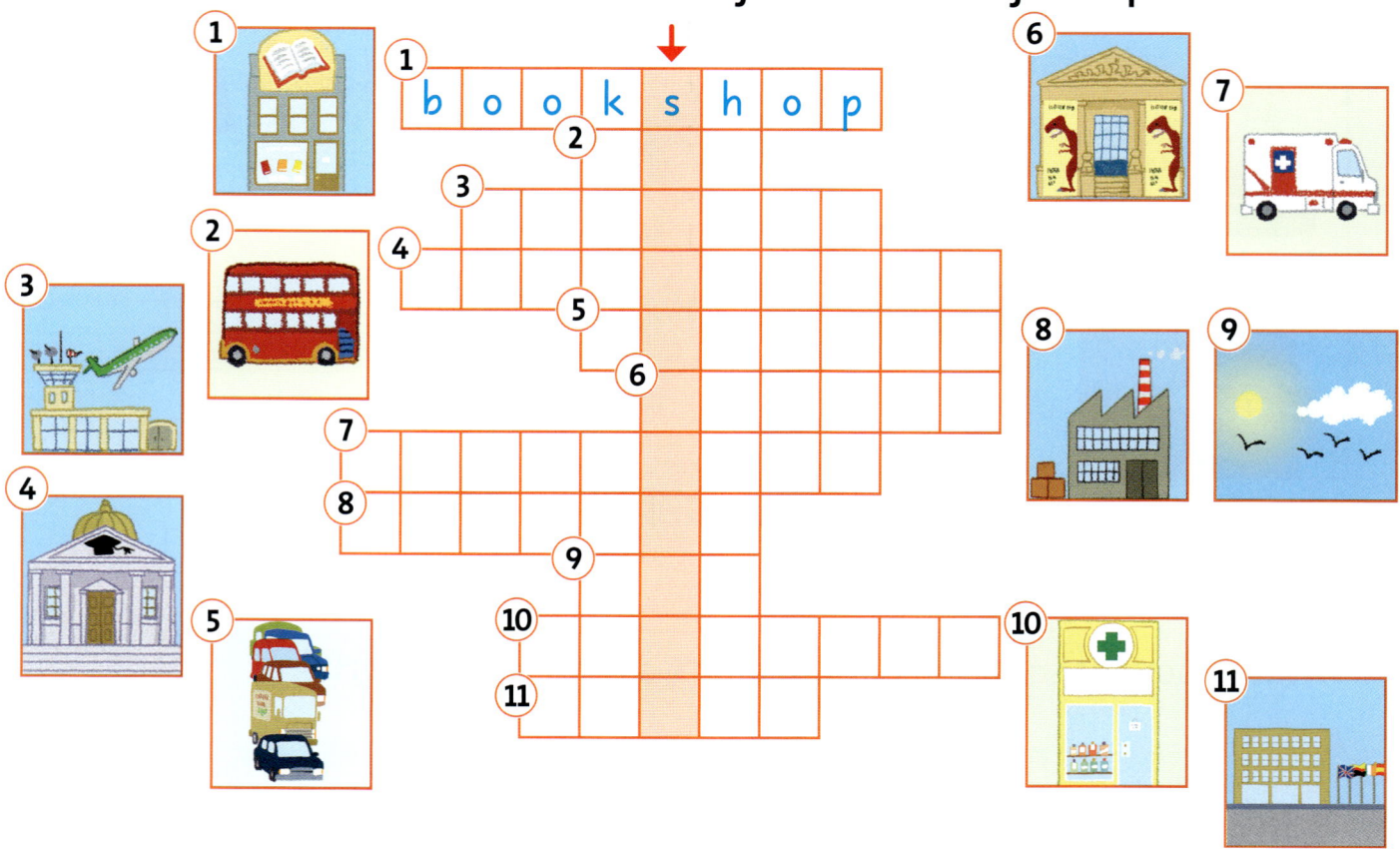

b o o k s h o p

Flyers practice test

Read the story. Choose a word from the box. Write the correct word next to numbers 1–5. There is one example.

Example		
~~caught~~	cheap	unhappy
buy	lovely	travelled
expensive	bought	sold

Yesterday, Mum wanted a train ticket and some other things from town, so I said 'No problem!' and I went shopping with my sister and brother. We __caught__ the bus into town and got off at the bus stop outside the supermarket. First we went to the shopping centre and we changed my shorts there because they were too small for me. Next we walked through the market. We didn't (1) _____ anything there though. After that we went to the post office. There we (2) _____ some stamps and posted some letters. We couldn't find any white envelopes for Mum but we did get a brush and comb from the chemist's next to the bookshop. They were quite cheap. Mum wanted some lemon soap for Grandma but there wasn't any. Then we collected a cake for Grandma's birthday. It was pink and it looked really (3) _____! After that, my brother got a computer game from a shop near the gym. It was very (4) _____ so we couldn't buy the train ticket for Mum. She was very (5) _____ about that!

(6) Now choose the best name for the story.

Tick one box.

A great bus trip ☐

A day in town ☐

At the shopping centre ☐

Flyers practice test

Look at the three pictures. Write about this story. Write 20 or more words.

_____

_____

_____

_____

Try to use these words in your story:

> family   stadium   baseball game
> hit the ball   catch the ball   steps

Flyers practice test

Listen and colour and write. There is one example. 🔊10

Adventure in the _____

3 Eating out

Words

1 Write the numbers for the things in Holly's kitchen.

salt	8	knife ☐	fork ☐	spoon ☐	chopsticks ☐
pizza ☐		pepper ☐	flour ☐	sugar ☐	olives ☐
butter ☐		jam ☐	honey ☐	yoghurt ☐	strawberries ☐

My best friend, Katy, is visiting me today. We're cooking in the kitchen!

2 Complete the sentences.

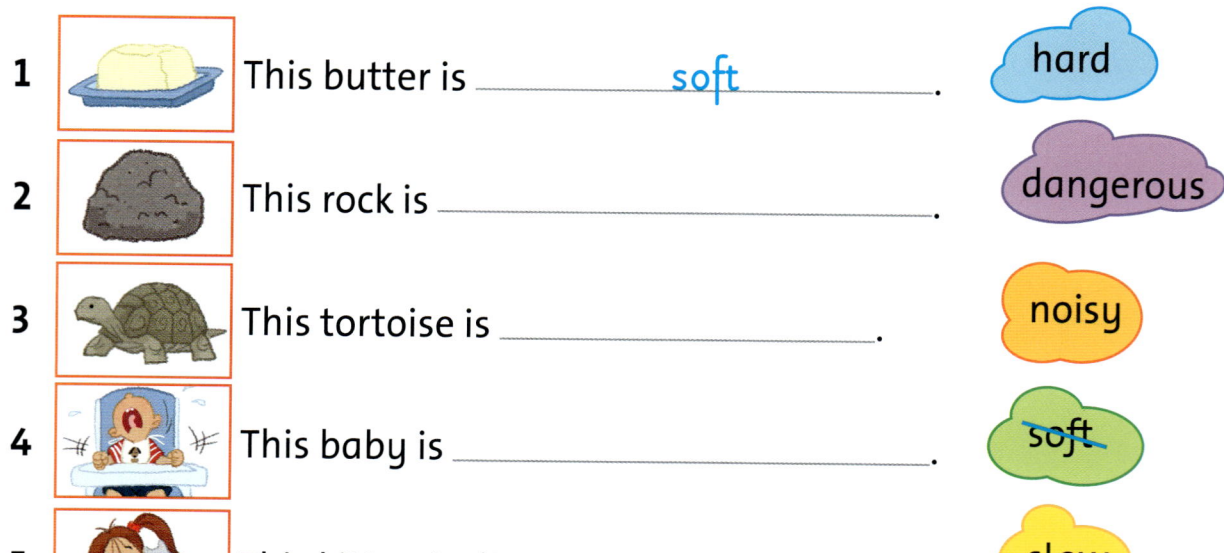

1 This butter is _____ soft _____ .

2 This rock is _____ .

3 This tortoise is _____ .

4 This baby is _____ .

5 This kitten isn't _____ .

hard

dangerous

noisy

~~soft~~

slow

UNIT 3 WORDS   pages 113–114

Story

1 Listen and read. Then act. 🔊11

1
Oh dear! I'm ill. I can't make lunch.
We'll make lunch today.

2
That smells like pizza.
Yes, and I think it's ready now!

3
And those look like biscuits.
Yes, they're chocolate biscuits.

4
Lovely! It tastes like Mum's pizza!
Yes, it's really good!

5
HOLLY! KATY!
Oh! That sounds like Mum!

6
This kitchen doesn't look like my kitchen!
Sorry, Mum.

2 Write the words in the sentences.

> smells   looks   feels   sounds   is   tastes

 1  2  3  4  5  6

1 Harry _____is_____ very like Holly. It's because they're twins.

2 That _____ like pizza cooking. I'm hungry!

3 That _____ like a baby. Emma's crying at the moment!

4 This _____ like wool. It's very soft!

5 That _____ like banana ice cream. I don't like it!

6 A tiger _____ like a cat, but it is dangerous.

GRAMMAR *be, look, sound, feel, taste, smell like* page 118   Unit 3   **21**

Speaking & listening

1 Play the 'feel it' game in small groups.

'It feels like…' means 'It feels similar to…'

It feels like an apple.

I think it feels like a ball.

2 Listen and draw lines. Which meal is not needed?

Yesterday it was Grandma's birthday!

Do you know what we ate?

Uncle Michael and our cousin Helen came. We all went for a meal in a restaurant!

1  2  3 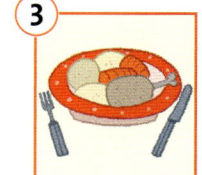 4  5

6  7  8  9  10

Words & speaking

1 **How does it feel? Complete the words in these sentences.**

1  When I smell pizzas it makes me h u n g r y.

2  When Grandma saw her amazing cake it made her h__ __ __.

3  When I eat too many biscuits it makes me i__ __.

4  When Emma saw her broken doll it made her s__ __.

5  When I have maths lessons it makes me b__ __ __ __.

6  When William spent all the money on computer games it made me a__ __ __ __.

7  When I lie down in the garden on a sunny day it makes me h__ __.

8  When Harry goes shopping in town all day it makes him t__ __ __ __.

9  When I'm by myself at night and I hear a strange noise, it makes me f__ __ __ __ __ __ __ __.

2 **How do these things make *you* feel? Tell a friend.**

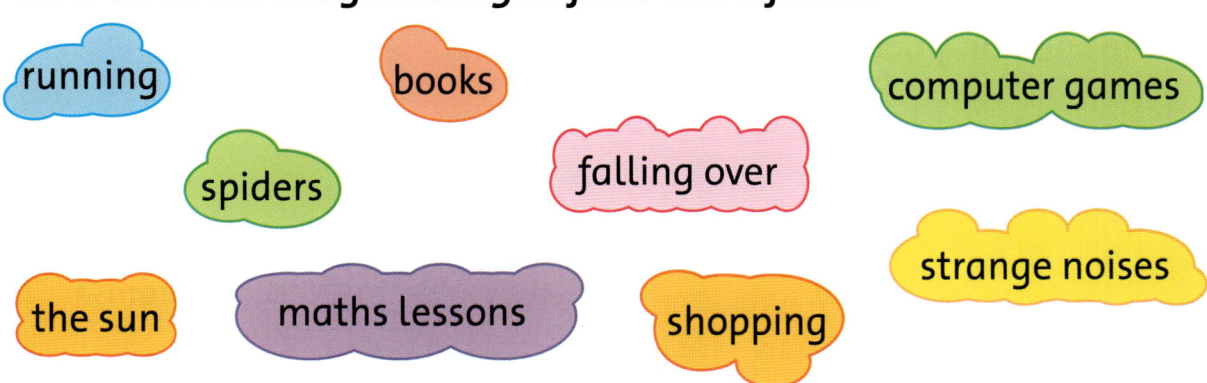

running books computer games

spiders falling over

strange noises

the sun maths lessons shopping

Words & speaking

1 **Complete the words under the pictures. Then find the pairs.**

1 h _a_ _t_

2 s ___ ___ s

3 e ___ ___ ___ ___ ___

4 b ___ ___ ___ ___

5 k ___ ___ ___ ___

6 b ___ ___ ___ ___

7 f ___ ___ ___

8 h ___ ___ ___ ___ ___

9 w ___ ___ ___ ___

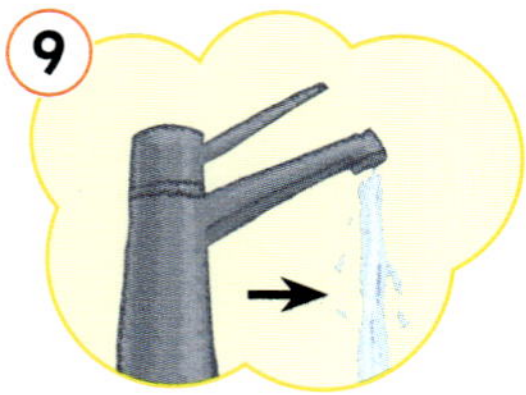

10 p ___ ___ ___ ___ ___

11 s ___ ___ ___

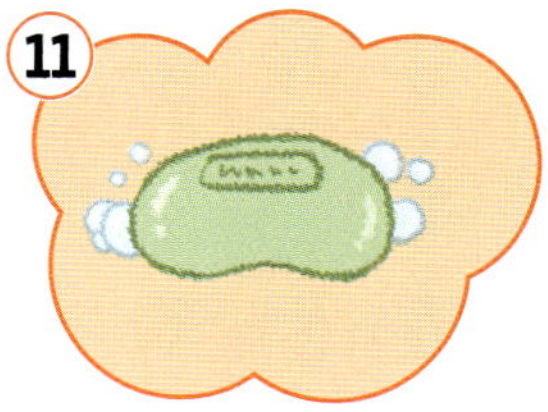

12 f ___ ___ ___

13 b ___ ___ ___ ___ ___

14 c ___ ___ ___ ___ ___

15 w ___ ___ ___

16 s ___ ___ ___ ___

17 s ___ ___ ___ s

18 c ___ ___ ___

19 s ___ ___ ___ ___

20 s ___ ___ ___

1	2	3	4	5	6	7	8	9	10
19									

2 **Do the speaking activity.** **P** 131

What's the first thing that I need?

You need 225 grams of butter.

Extended reading: Holly's diary

1 Read Holly's diary. Order the pictures.

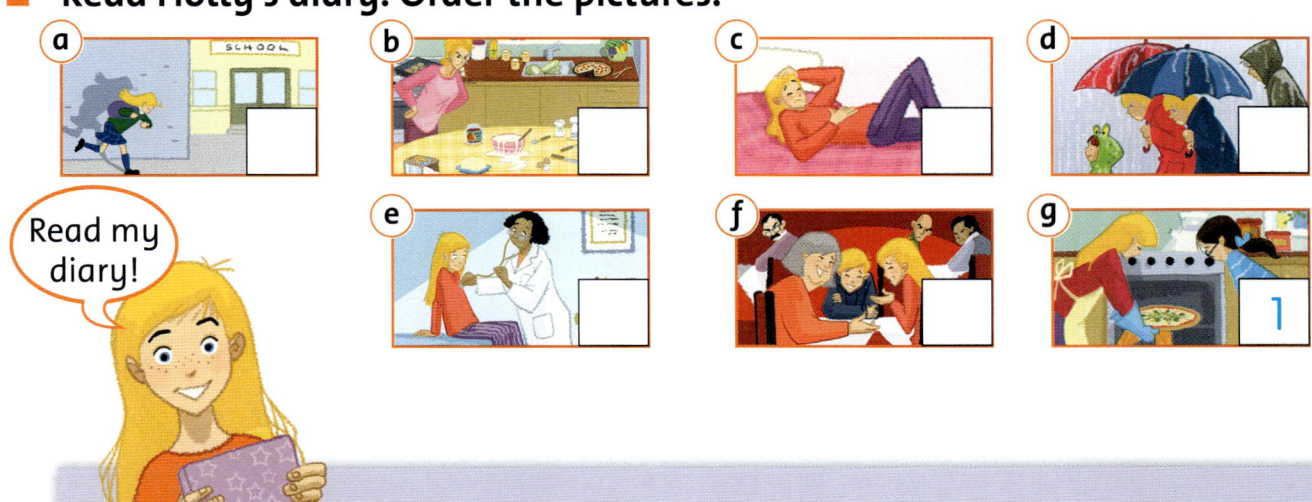

a

b

c

d

Read my diary!

e

f

g [1]

16th March

Dear Diary

On Saturday afternoon my best friend, Katy, came to my house and we did some cooking. We made pizzas with olives on them, and biscuits, too! When we finished, the kitchen was very **(1)** _untidy_ and that made Mum a bit **(2)** _____!

Then, on Sunday all the family went out for lunch. It was a surprise for Grandma's 80th birthday! Going to the restaurant made Harry and I feel very **(3)** _____. We couldn't wait to go! We don't often go to restaurants, you see. We walked to the restaurant and the rain on the way made us **(4)** _____, but we didn't mind because we had umbrellas. In the restaurant we laughed and talked a lot and I think we were a bit too **(5)** _____. That was because we had to wait a long time for our food. The smell of the pizza made us very **(6)** _____.

Then the food arrived! I had soup and I ate lots and lots of pizza too, because it tasted **(7)** _____. But that evening all those pieces of pizza made me **(8)** _____. This morning Mum took me to the doctor's. The doctor was very **(9)** _____. She gave me some medicine for my stomach and that made me feel **(10)** _____. But that meant I was a bit **(11)** _____ for school again and I felt **(12)** _____ about that! But when I got there the teacher just said 'No problem!'.

pizza
olives

2 Read the diary again and write the missing words.

ill ~~untidy~~ better delicious late friendly
hungry wet worried angry excited noisy

Flyers practice test

Listen and tick (✓) the box. There is one example. 🔊⑬

What time did the lesson start?

A 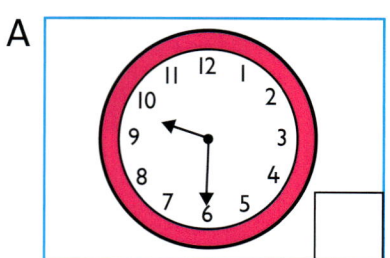 B 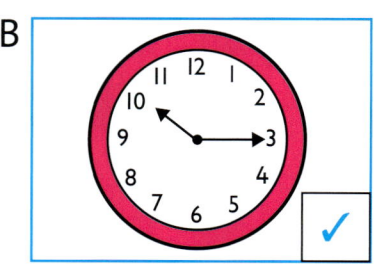 C

1 What is Betty making in her cooking lesson today?

A  B  C

2 What should Betty get from the fridge?

A  B  C

3 What does Betty need to do next?

A  B  C

4 What did Betty forget to do?

A  B  C

Flyers practice test

Sophia is talking to her brother, Oliver. Read the conversation and choose the best answer. Write a letter (A–H) for each answer. You do not need to use all the letters.

Example

Sophia:	What shall we get Mum for her birthday?
Oliver:	_____ A

Questions

1 Sophia: Where should we buy one from?

Oliver: _____

2 Sophia: OK. Let's catch a train. What platform is it?

Oliver: _____

3 Sophia: Have you got any money?

Oliver: _____

4 Sophia: How shall we pay for our tickets, then?

Oliver: _____

5 Sophia: We can't do that! Do you want to go tomorrow, instead?

Oliver: _____

(Example)

A I think she'd like a bracelet.

B I think it's platform 2.

C Ok! Good idea.

D Let's ask Mum for some.

E Haven't you got one?

F Oh no, I don't think I have!

G I didn't go there.

H We could go to the city centre.

4 At school

Words

1 Find the school subjects and colour the lines.

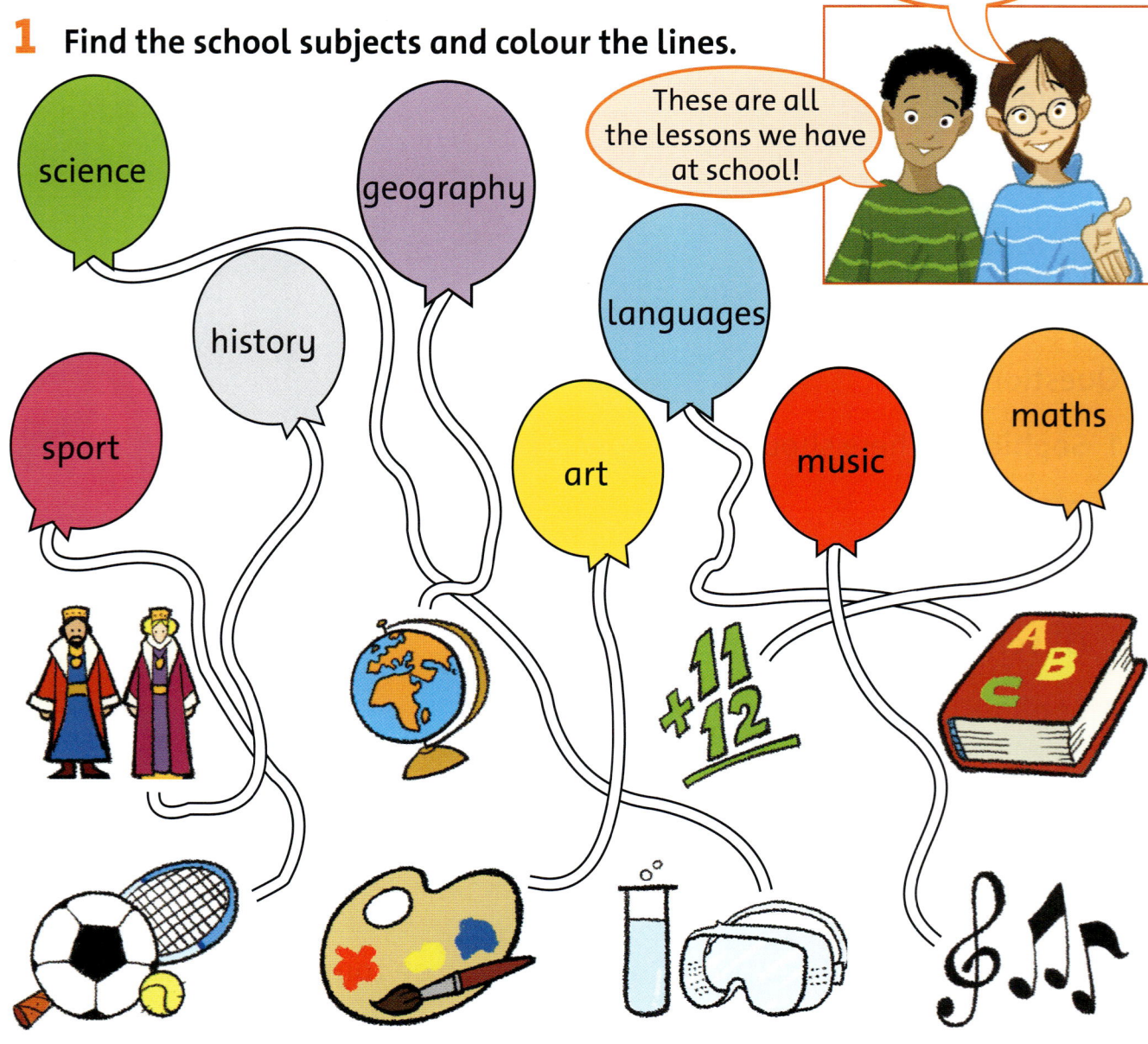

We've got lots of different subjects!

These are all the lessons we have at school!

science

geography

history

languages

sport

art

music

maths

2 Which subject has got the longest line? _____

3 Tell your friend about the subjects you do at school.

Which subjects do you like? Why?

Which subjects are difficult? Why?

What's your favourite subject? Why?

Which subjects do you have tests in? How do tests make you feel?

Story

1 Listen and read. Then act. 🔊14

1 What are you doing? It's midnight!

I couldn't sleep.

2 Emma, it's four o'clock in the morning. Go to sleep!

3 It's quarter past seven. Time to get up!

I'm very tired.

4 What time is it? Are we late again?

I'm not sure... Oh, it's quarter to nine. Let's run.

5 It's midday.

What's the matter? Don't you want to play?

Sorry, I'm really tired!

6 Dinner time! Oh dear, Holly's sleeping and it's only half past six!

2 Match the clocks with the pictures in the story. Write numbers.

☐ 1   ☐   ☐   ☐   ☐   ☐

3 Think about your day. Draw the times on these clocks. Then talk to a friend.

Midday is 12 o'clock in the day, and midnight is 12 o'clock at night.

GRAMMAR *What time...?* page 118

Writing

1 **Write the days onto the timetable.**

Harry's timetable					
M _____	T _____	W**ednesday**	T _____	F _____

a.m.   morning lessons

morning break

lunch break

p.m.   afternoon lessons

after-school clubs

2 **Look at the timetable. Write the answers to these questions.**

1   What time is lunch every day? It's at ____**midday / twelve o'clock**____ .

2   What time is the IT lesson on Monday? It's at _____ .

3   What time does art club start on Wednesday?

   It's after school at _____

4   How many language lessons are there each week? _____

5   How long is morning break each day? _____

3 **Now ask questions about Harry's timetable.**

Words & listening

1 Work alone. Use a dictionary to find the meanings. Then work with two friends. Tell your friends what the words on your list mean.

Student A	Student B	Student C
to borrow	a program	frightened
to improve	the past	excellent
to join	a club	easy
to repeat	a butterfly	difficult
to teach	a beetle	lazy

2 Katy and Holly are talking about school. Draw lines to make sentences. Listen and check. 🔊15

1 The teachers think doing homework
2 Katy arrives at school at
3 When Harry had to see the teacher he felt
4 The science teacher says William is
5 William thinks maths is
6 Katy's teacher thinks her maths
7 Harry's maths teacher says he's
8 Last week Holly joined the
9 Katy says she has to repeat words after the teacher
10 Holly doesn't like history because she
11 Katy loves her school because she's got

a very lazy.
b quarter to nine.
c lots of friends there.
d a very easy subject.
e is improving.
f is very important.
g art club.
h an excellent student.
i thinks it's difficult.
j in language lessons.
k a bit frightened.

3 Do the speaking activity. P132

I think this picture goes with this information.

Yes, I agree and that goes first.

Words

1 Look at Harry's school work. Join the words with the pictures. What are these things made of? Write the words in the correct boxes.

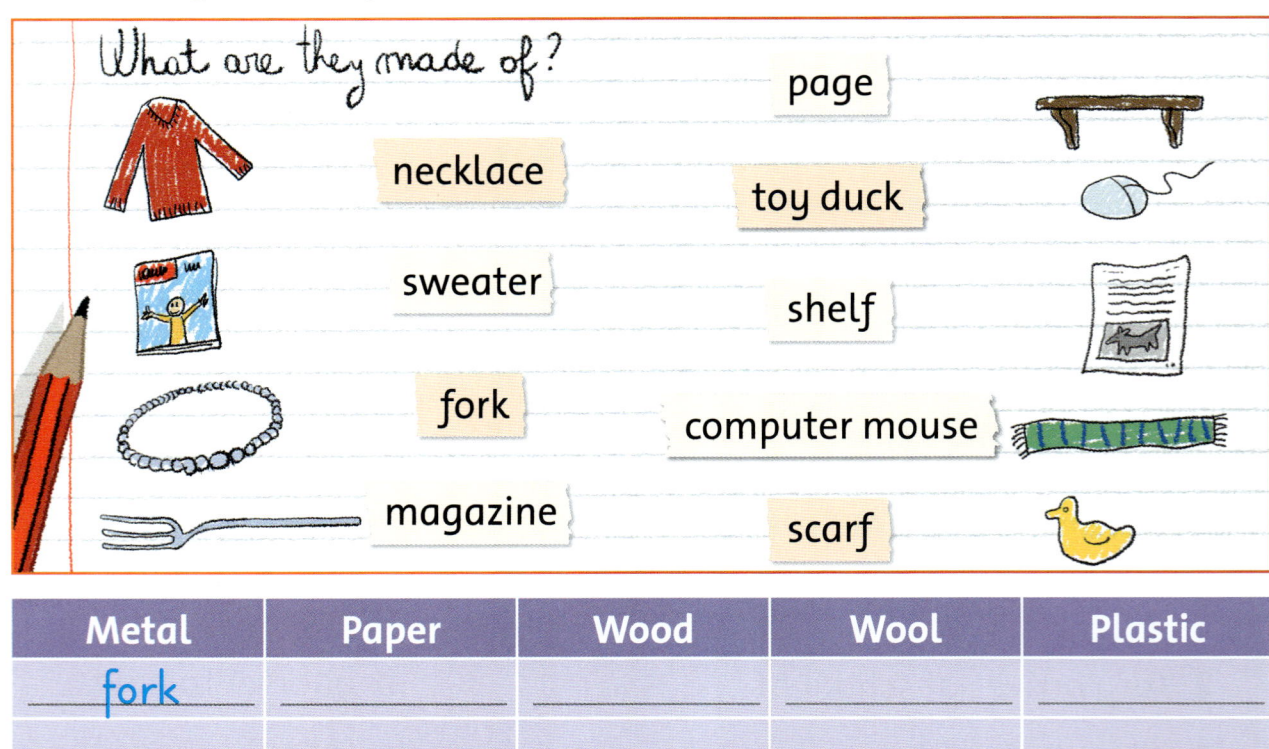

What are they made of?

necklace

sweater

fork

magazine

page

toy duck

shelf

computer mouse

scarf

Metal	Paper	Wood	Wool	Plastic
fork				

2 Make the word wall! Read and write the words in the puzzle.

not ~~paper (4)~~

very, very good (9)

a beautiful insect (9)

English is one (8)

Say it again, please! (6)

lunch time! (6)

very, very big (8)

not plastic (5)

get better at it (7)

a.m. (7)

things you learn (5)

not early (4)

afraid (10)

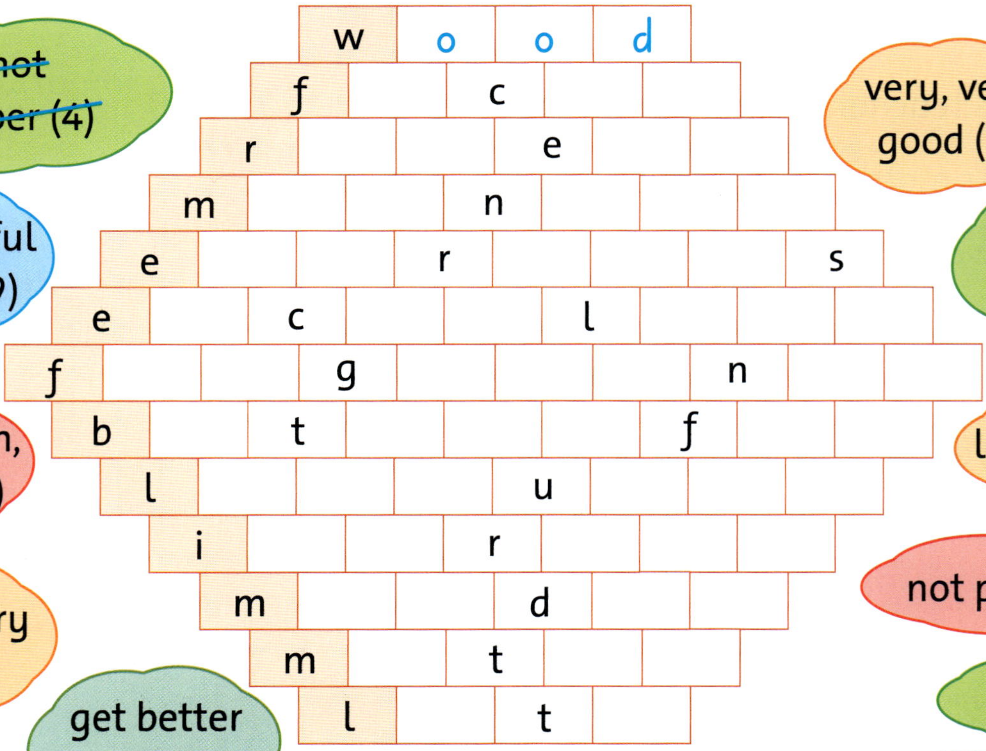

w o o d
f c
r e
m n
e r s
e c l
f g n
b t f
l u
i r
m d
m t
l t

Flyers practice test

Read the story. Choose a word from the box. Write the correct word next to numbers 1–5. There is one example.

Example				
~~had~~	would	learnt	excellent	tell
gave	excited	expensive	told	

Hello, I'm Harry and today it's Thursday. I didn't have a very good morning. At half past ten (which was during my break time) I ___had___ to go and see my geography teacher. He said it was because I was talking in the classroom but actually, it was my friend, David. I didn't (**1**) _____ the geography teacher that.

This afternoon, in our history lesson we (**2**) _____ all about castles. It was a very interesting lesson. And after the class, the teacher (**3**) _____ us a letter for our parents. I read it on my way home. What a big surprise! We're going to go on a school trip to a castle! I gave the letter to Mum and Dad when I got home this evening. My sister, Holly, had the same letter. We were really (**4**) _____ about it. Dad was a bit unhappy. He said the trip was too (**5**) _____ ! Then Mum read the letter carefully and she thought it would be good for us to go on a trip with friends. She said 'You can go if you want!' It's eight weeks until we go. I can't wait!

(**6**) **Now choose the best name for the story.**
  Tick one box.

Harry's good news ☐

Harry's good day ☐

Harry's good friend ☐

Flyers practice test

Listen and write. There is one example. 🔊16

Art Club

What day?	<u>Wednesday</u> after school
1 Teacher's name:	Mrs _____
2 Where is it?	opposite the school _____
3 Number of students this year:	_____
4 Next week – making:	_____
5 Expensive?	_____ for this year

Flyers practice test

Look and read. Choose the correct words and write them on the lines. There is one example.

a platform   invitations   an eagle   strawberries

wool

When you play golf, you hit balls into these. Creatures live under the ground in these too. ___holes___

yoghurt

1 This is a very slow animal with a shell on its back. _____

2 This is a kind of game. Someone asks you questions to find out what you know. _____

holes

3 These are times when people dress up in costumes, sing, dance and have fun. _____

projects

4 A subject you study using a computer. _____

5 You eat this in a bowl with a spoon. It's white and you sometimes have fruit in it. _____

a gym

6 You stand here when you're waiting for a train. _____

a quiz

7 This is a large bird with big wings. It catches and eats small creatures. _____

8 You do these alone or in groups. They help you to learn more about a subject. _____

IT

9 You go to this building to do exercise or sport. _____

surprises

10 You get these letters when your friends ask you to go to a party. _____

a motorway   a tortoise   festivals

Revision 1

1 Read the words and write the opposites in the crossword.

Across →

2 late

5 tidy

7 cheap

8 good

Down ↓

1 interesting

2 full

3 hard

4 noisy

6 ugly

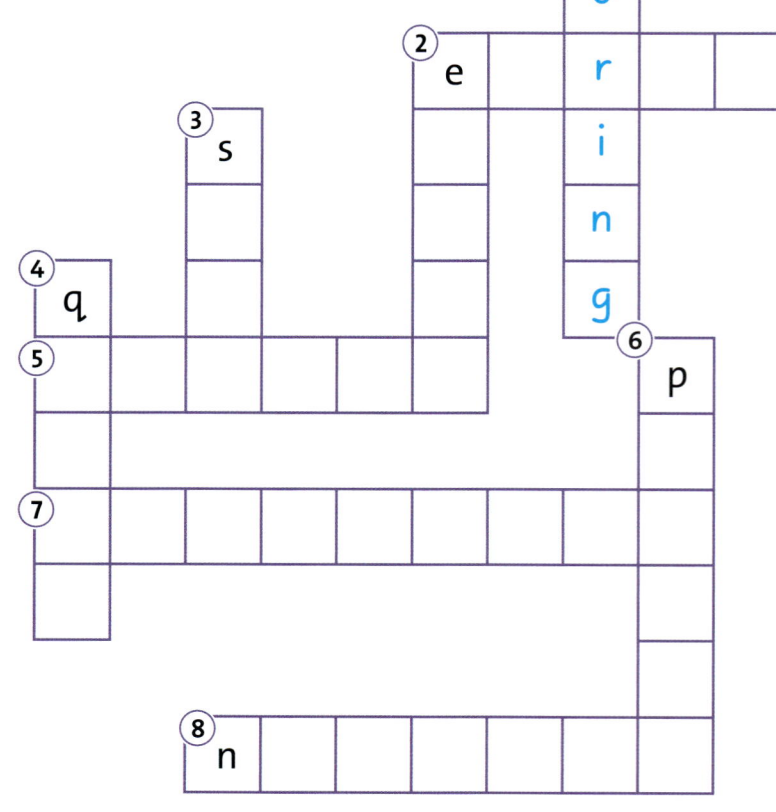

1 b
o
2 e | r
3 s | i
n
4 q | g
5 | 6 p
7
8 n

2 Order the letters. What are they made of? Draw lines.

1
v e e
n l o
p e

e n v e l o p e

2
k e
f n i
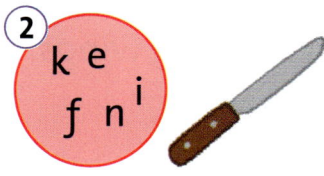

___ ___ ___ ___ ___

3
a s
r c f

___ ___ ___ ___ ___

 metal
 paper
plastic
 wool
 wood

4
u d
k
c
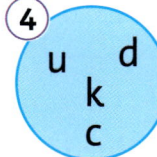

___ ___ ___ ___

5
k
d e
s
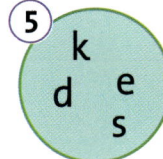

___ ___ ___ ___

6
k o
o b
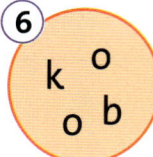

___ ___ ___ ___

3 Complete the dialogue.

~~everything~~ anything everywhere nothing everyone something No-one

Mum, when you go to town, will you buy a present for my friend, Helen? It's her party this afternoon.

OK, Katy, I'll do my best.

Katy's mum is back at home now.

Mum: I've got (**1**) *everything* I need from town!

Katy: And did you get a present for Helen, Mum?

Mum: I'm really sorry, Katy. I looked (**2**) _____ but I couldn't find (**3**) _____ for Helen.

Katy: I don't want to go to the party then, Mum. I've got (**4**) _____ to give her! (**5**) _____ goes to a party without a present, Mum!

Mum: Don't worry. Go and see (**6**) _____ at the party and have a good time. I'll get (**7**) _____ for Katy and you can give it to her at the end if you want.

Katy: Ok, thanks Mum!

Mum: No problem!

4 Draw the times on the clocks. Then draw lines to *a.m.* or *p.m.*

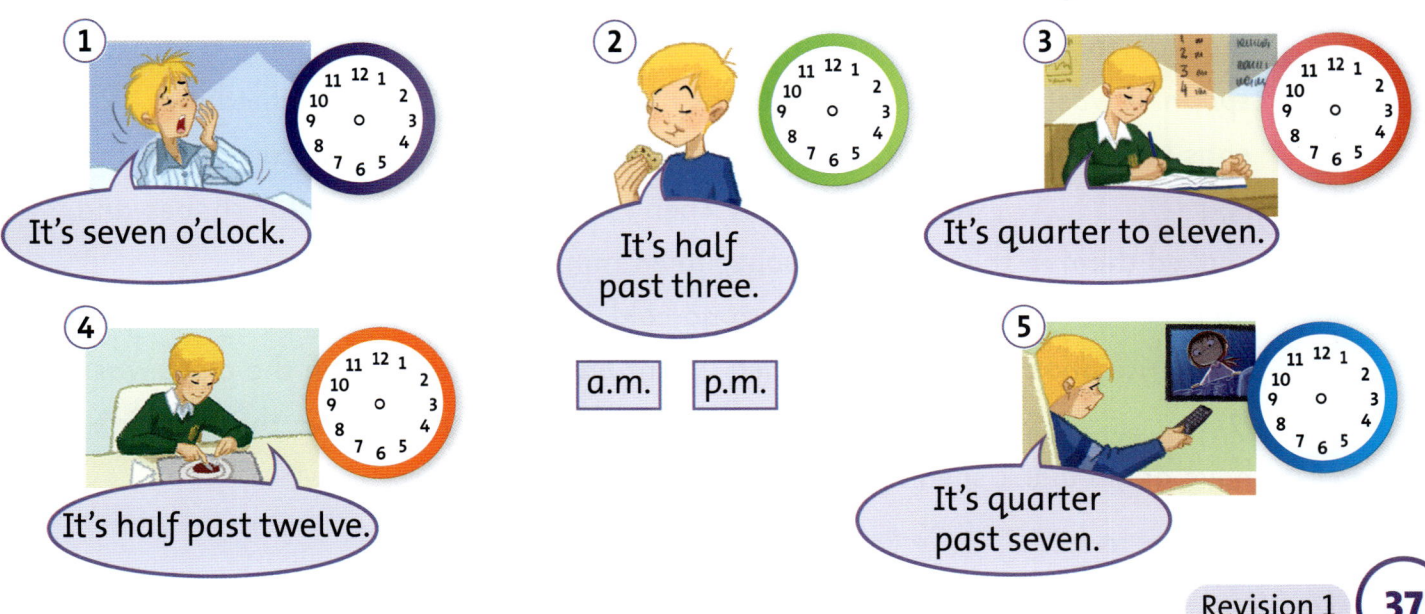

1 It's seven o'clock.

2 It's half past three.

3 It's quarter to eleven.

4 It's half past twelve.

5 It's quarter past seven.

a.m.   p.m.

5 Listen and draw lines. 🔊17

① ② ③ ④ ⑤ ⑥

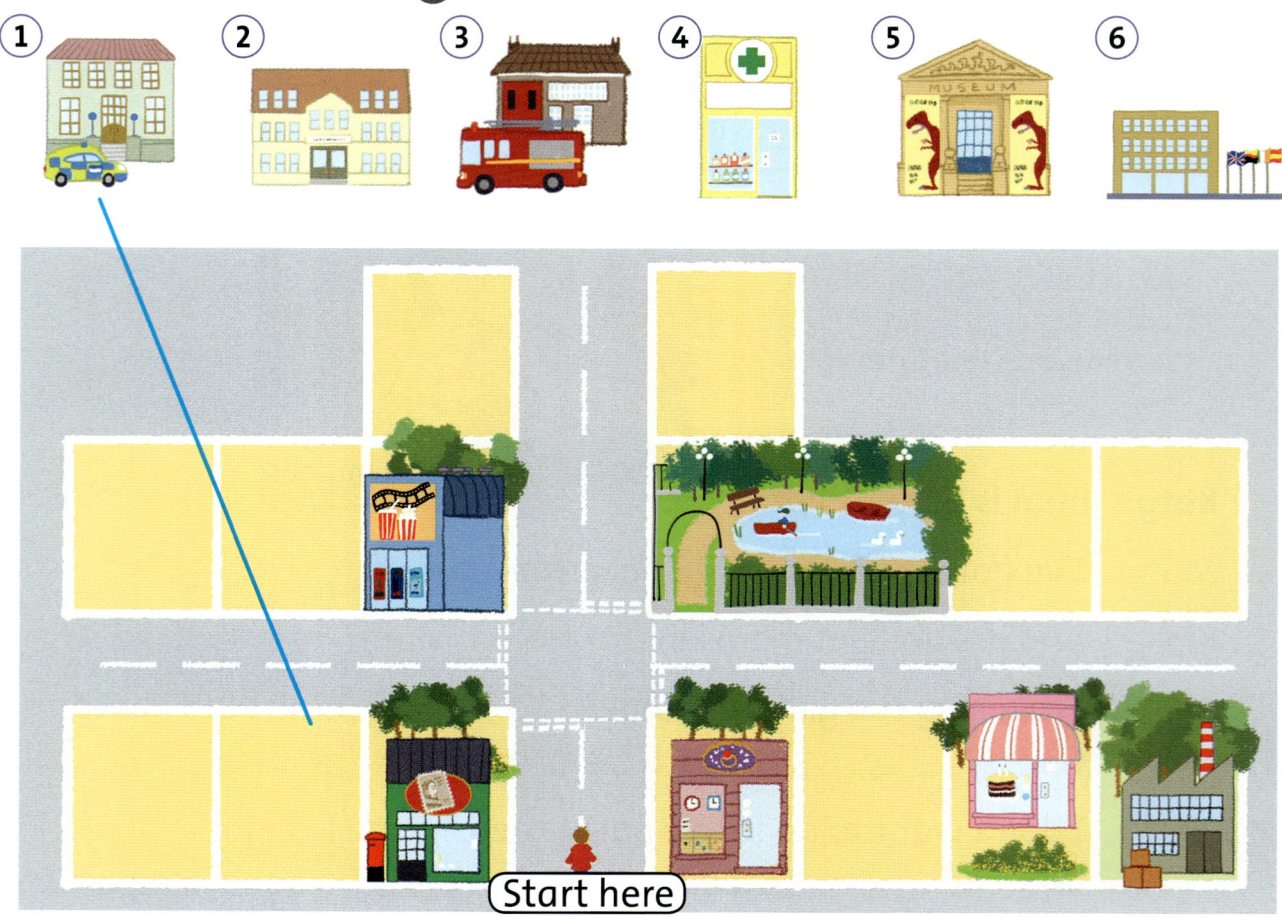

Start here

6 Read Holly's diary and write the missing words.

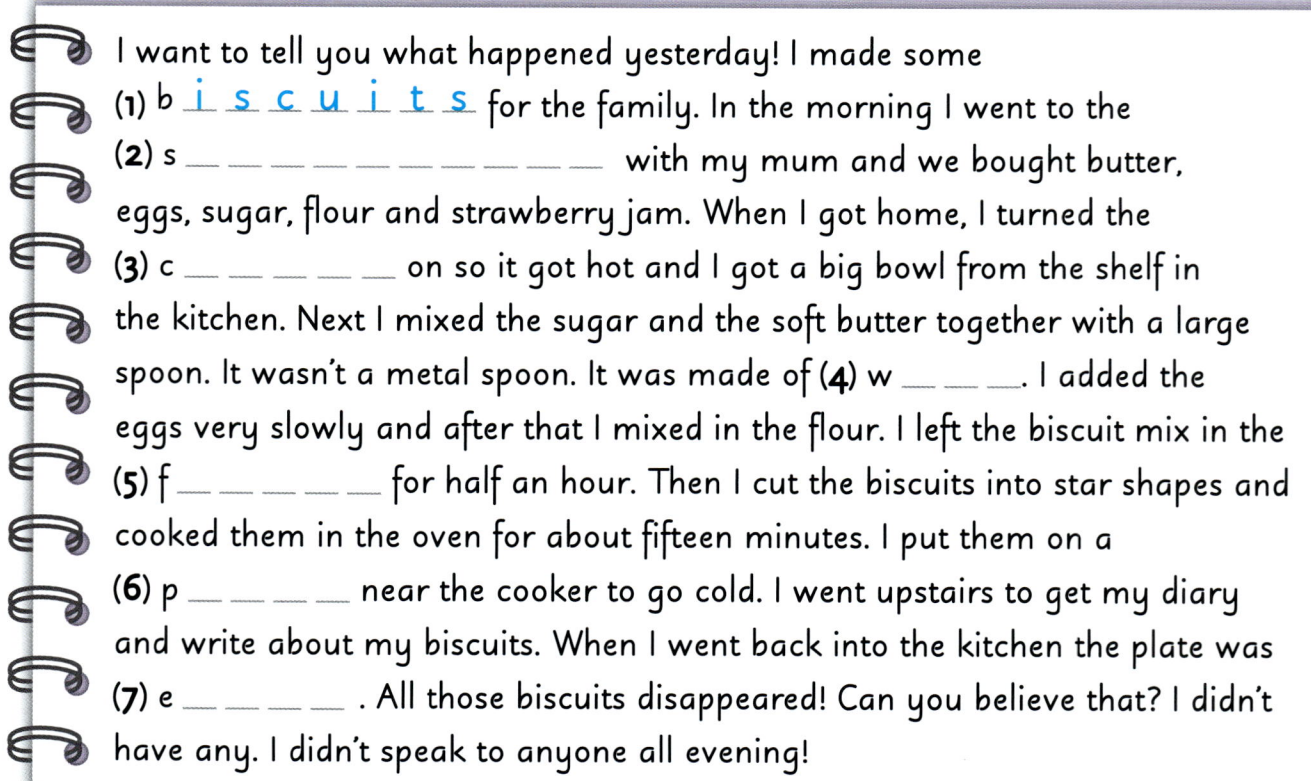

I want to tell you what happened yesterday! I made some
(1) b i s c u i t s for the family. In the morning I went to the
(2) s _ _ _ _ _ _ _ _ _ _ _ _ _ _ with my mum and we bought butter,
eggs, sugar, flour and strawberry jam. When I got home, I turned the
(3) c _ _ _ _ _ _ on so it got hot and I got a big bowl from the shelf in
the kitchen. Next I mixed the sugar and the soft butter together with a large
spoon. It wasn't a metal spoon. It was made of (4) w _ _ _ _. I added the
eggs very slowly and after that I mixed in the flour. I left the biscuit mix in the
(5) f _ _ _ _ _ _ for half an hour. Then I cut the biscuits into star shapes and
cooked them in the oven for about fifteen minutes. I put them on a
(6) p _ _ _ _ _ near the cooker to go cold. I went upstairs to get my diary
and write about my biscuits. When I went back into the kitchen the plate was
(7) e _ _ _ _ _ . All those biscuits disappeared! Can you believe that? I didn't
have any. I didn't speak to anyone all evening!

1 These pictures tell a story. It's called 'Mrs Hall's shopping trip'. Look at the example for picture 1. Now you tell the story.

> Mr Hall is going to work and his wife is going to town. She wants to buy a new phone. She's leaving the house now, but her key is on the shelf in the hall.

2 Ask and answer about the things you do in town.

3 Find ten more differences. Talk to your friend about the pictures.

4 Now do the Speaking test. **P** 123–124

5 A day out

Words

1 Complete the words. Draw lines to match the things to the places.

~~seats~~ pyramids dinosaurs actors clowns
wild animals screen cartoons swing stage cage

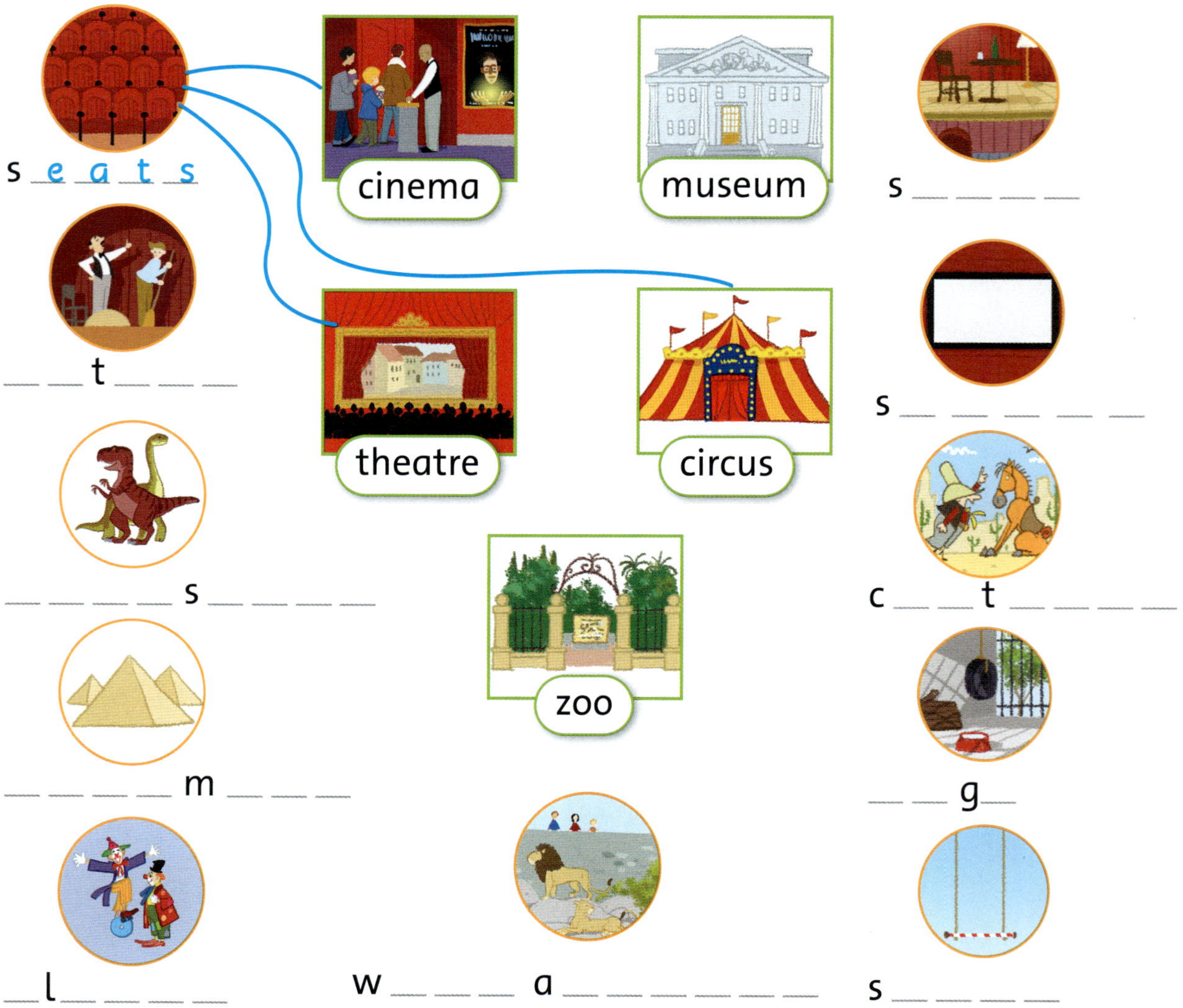

s _e_ _a_ _t_ _s_

cinema

museum

s _ _ _ _ _

_ _ t _ _ _

theatre

circus

s _ _ _ _ _

_ _ _ _ s _ _ _

zoo

c _ _ t _ _ _ _

_ _ _ _ m _ _ _

_ l _ _ _ _ _

w _ _ _ a _ _ _ _ _ _ _

_ _ g _

s _ _ _ _

2 Write the words under the pictures.

evening afternoon night morning

1
_____

2
_____

3
_____

4
_____

Conversation

1 Tomorrow Mrs Brown is going to take the children on a special day out. Read the conversation and choose the best question or answer.

Holly: b

1 Mrs Brown: Shall we go to the museum in the morning? They've got some interesting dinosaurs there.

Holly: ▢

2 Mrs Brown: OK then, let's go to the museum in the morning.

Harry: ▢

3 Mrs Brown: Quite early ... at half past eight. So, let's do that in the morning! And in the afternoon shall we go to the theatre?

Harry: ▢

4 Mrs Brown: Well, we could go to the cinema and see a film instead.

Emma: ▢

5 Mrs Brown: That's a good idea. There's a very funny one which begins at quarter past two.

Holly: ▢

6 Mrs Brown: Two hours. And in the evening there's a circus on in town! Shall we go there?

Harry: ▢

7 Mrs Brown: The circus ends at half past ten in the evening. It's going to be a special day! Are you going to come with us, William?

William: ▢

a Oh yes please! I'd really like to see the clowns.

b ~~Where are we going to go on our day out, Mum?~~

c No, I'm not!

d Can we see a cartoon? I love them!

e Oh, I really want to see them! Let's go there!

f What time does the museum open?

g Oh, I hate going there! It's boring!

h And how long is the cartoon?

2 Draw the times on the clocks.

Museum opens   Cartoon starts

Cartoon finishes   Circus finishes

Listening

1 What's William going to do tomorrow? Listen and number five of the pictures. 🔊18

2 Can you remember what William is going to do? Draw lines and make sentences.

William is going to / William isn't going to	stay	to	in his bedroom.
	cook	a shower	the museum.
	watch	his homework	until eleven o'clock.
	go	some computer games	television programmes.
	do	in bed	for everyone.
	have	several	at the shopping centre.
	buy	dinner	before he goes out.

GRAMMAR *be going to* page 119

Writing & speaking

Remember! We don't change the verb after 'going to'.

1 Write about what you're going to do tomorrow.

I'm going to _____

_____ .

In the morning I'm going to _____

and _____ .

In the afternoon I'm going to _____

and _____ .

In the evening I'm going to _____

and _____ .

2 Match the pictures and the sentences.

1 That's very cheap!   **e**

2 They're extinct now!

3 That's interesting!

4 That's exciting!

5 That's excellent!

6 That's very high!

7 That's very brave!

8 They're expensive!

3 Do the speaking activity. **P 133**

Words

1 Make the word wall! Read the sentences and write the answers in the puzzle.

Puzzle rows:
a _ _ _ _ n _ _ n
b _ _ _ e _ _ t
c _ _ _ _ o
c e r e a l
o _ _ n
w _ _ d
g _ _
e _ _
s _ a _
s _ _ g _
o _ _ v _ _
s _ _ _ p _
s _ _ p _ i _ _
g _ o _ _ _ _ p

People have this with milk for breakfast. (6)

They're on pizzas. They're green or black. (6)

You can open doors with it. (3)

Something you don't know about that's exciting. (8)

You sit on it. (4)

It's after midday (9)

Like a necklace but smaller. (8)

Like the sea, but much bigger. (5)

A children's film. (7)

A school subject about hills, rivers and lakes! (9)

You wash your hair with this. (7)

A place where you play sport. (3)

Animals that live in the jungle. (4)

At the theatre you can see actors on this. (5)

2 Join the word halves to find words for things you find in a house.

1 _window_
2 _____
3 _____
4 _____
5 _____
6 _____
7 _____

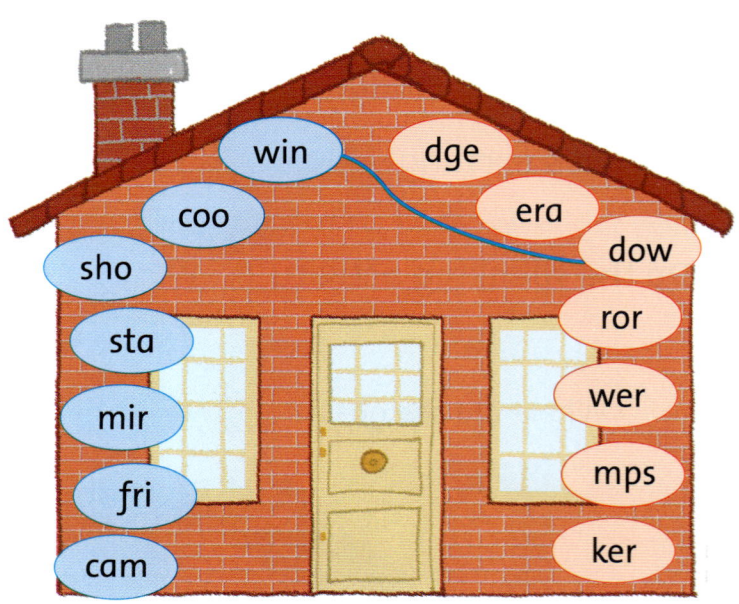

win   dge
coo   era
sho   dow
sta   ror
mir   wer
fri   mps
cam   ker

Extended reading: Holly's diary

1 **Read Holly's diary. Write the missing words.**

late	~~excited~~	expensive	brave	interesting
extinct	high	excellent	bored	empty

Read my diary!

April 20th

Dear Diary,

We had a really amazing time today! Mum took us all on a trip. We were very **(1)** _excited_ about that. First we went to the 🏛 in town. We saw some 🦕 there and I found out a lot about them for my school project. They became **(2)** _____ millions of years ago! There was also a lot of very **(3)** _____ information about the 🔺. You can visit them in the 🏜 in a country called Egypt.

Then, in the afternoon, we went to cinema and saw a 🎬 about some friendly monsters. I think George and Harry were a bit **(4)** _____ because the film was for young children. Emma thought the monsters were a bit frightening. We got good 🪑 because the cinema was nearly **(5)** _____!

Then, in the evening we went to the 🎪. But before that we went to a 🍔 for a meal. I loved the food. It was **(6)** _____! I felt sorry for Mum because it was quite **(7)** _____ and she had to pay for everything. My favourite part of the day was the 🎪! There was a woman on a big 🔲. She flew through the air and a man caught her. I thought she'd fall. She was very **(8)** _____ up in the air and she was so **(9)** _____ to go all the way up there! Well, it's very **(10)** _____ now – it's nearly 🕐 and I'm going to go to bed!

2 **Take it in turns to read a sentence from Holly's diary. Say the words for the pictures.**

Flyers practice test

Listen and colour and write. There is one example. 🔊19

_____ please

Flyers practice test

Look at the three pictures. Write about this story. Write 20 or more words.

_____

_____

_____

_____

Try to use these words in your story:

skateboarding   hill   hole   rabbit   surprised   disappear   laugh

6 Dream jobs

Words

1 **Write the words under the pictures.**

~~artist~~ photographer teacher manager singer tennis player
police officer designer journalist mechanic dentist engineer

1
| a | r | t | i | s | t |

2
| | | h | | | | |

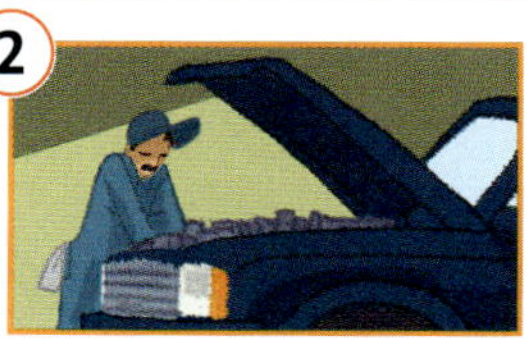

3
| | | s | | | | |

4
| | | g | | | | | |

5
| | | | | | s | |

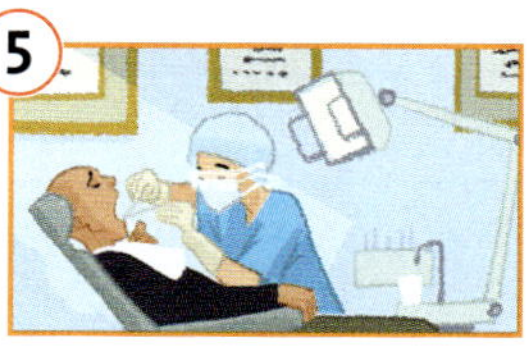

6
| | | u | | | | | | | |

7
| | n | | | |

8
| | | a | | | |

9
| | | | | | | | | p | | | |

10
| | | | | | s | |
| | | a | | | |

11
| | | | | c | |
| | f | | | | | |

12
| | | | | h | |

2 **Which job would you like to do? Which job wouldn't you like to do? Why? Talk to a friend about it.**

I'd like to be an artist because I love drawing.

I wouldn't like to be a police officer because they have to wear a uniform. I hate my school uniform!

UNIT 6
WORDS   page 115

Words & speaking

1 Draw lines to match the words with the pictures.

office

classroom

restaurant

hospital

fire station

kitchen

police station

airport

circus

theatre

2 Look in your dictionary for these jobs. Ask and answer.

pilot   waiter   doctor   fire fighter   clown   actor
police officer   cook   teacher   manager

Where does a waiter work, Holly?

In a restaurant.

3 Do the speaking activity. **P** 134

He works in a hospital. He helps people who are ill.

A doctor!

That's right.

Story

1 Listen and read. Then act. 🔊20

1 For homework, I'd like you to write about your dream job.

2 Footballers are rich. But I'm not good at football …

3 I'd like to go to university. But students are poor …

4 I could be an engineer and build high bridges. But I'm a bit lazy.

5 Harry? Are you listening? Do you know what you have to do?

6 Yes, Mr Black. It's easy! I've got lots of ideas.

Mr Black's very kind and friendly. I'd like to be a teacher!

2 Write the words under the pictures.

> lazy   rich   poor   brave

a

b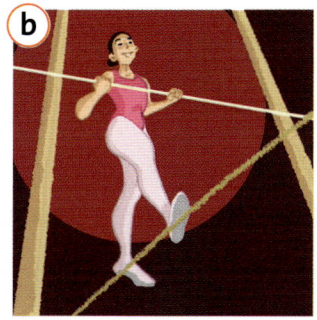

c

d

_____   _____   _____   _____

Writing & listening

1 The children are talking together about the jobs their parents do. Put the **words** next to the pictures and write **verbs** in the spaces.

~~journalist~~ businesswoman office newspaper meetings night

make**s** ~~work**s**~~ write**s** travel**s**

Look! We add 's' to the verb for **he**, **she** and **it**.

George: What does your dad do, Katy?

Katy: He's a (**1**) _journalist_. He (**2**) _works_ in an

(**3**) _____ and he (**4**) _____ stories for a

(**5**) _____. Sometimes he's at work during the

(**6**) _____.

George: And what about your mum?

Katy: She's a (**7**) _____. She has lots of

important (**8**) _____ to go to. She (**9**) _____

to other towns for her work.

2 Listen to the children and write the jobs under the people. 🔊21

dentist photographer engineer ~~businessman~~ farmer artist nurse

Holly and Harry's dad

George's mum

George's dad

businessman _____ _____

Helen's mum

Helen's dad

David's mum

David's dad

_____ _____ _____ _____

Words

1 Write the words in the puzzle to find the name of the job in the picture.

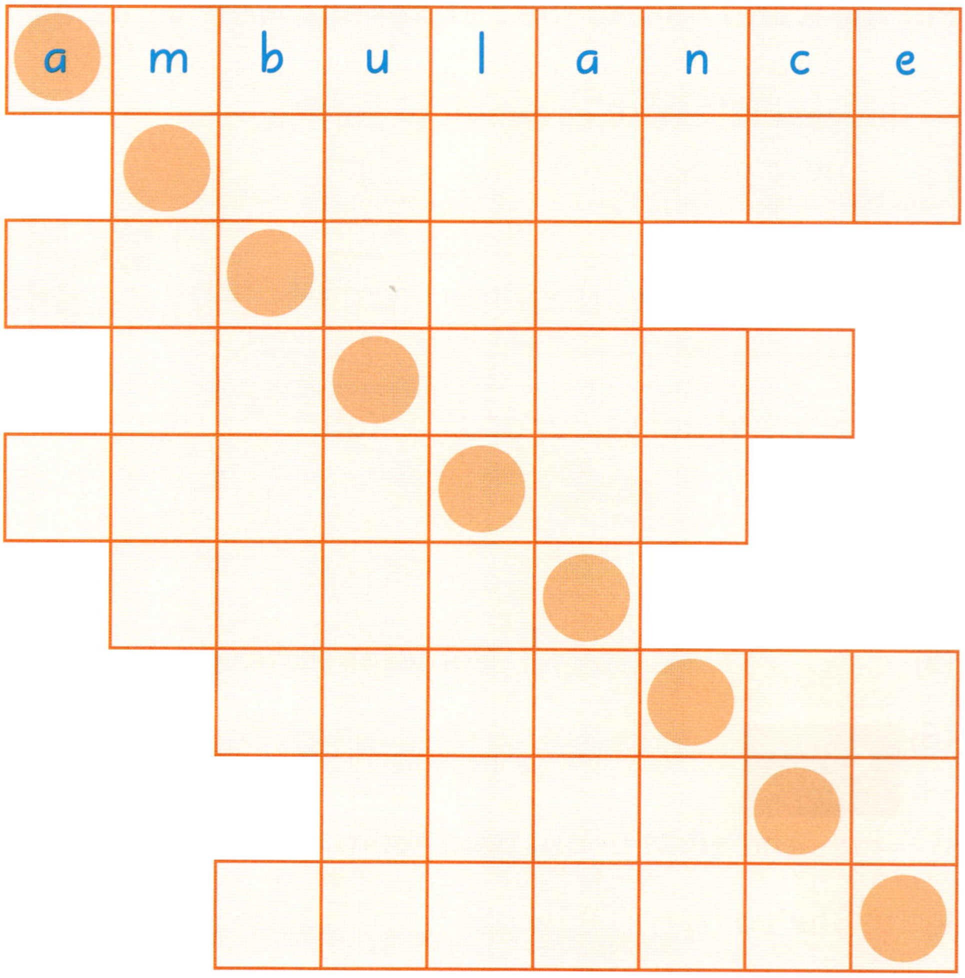

1. | a | m | b | u | l | a | n | c | e |

Hi! I'm an

a_____ _____ _____ _____

2 Join the word halves to find the places where people work.

| sch | ho | fact | off | cir | restau | thea | hosp |

| ice | cus | ital | rant | tre | ory | ool | tel |

1 school 3 _____ 5 _____ 7 _____

2 _____ 4 _____ 6 _____ 8 _____

UNIT 6 WORDS page 115

Flyers practice test

Where do Betty and her family work?
Listen and write a letter in each box. There is one example. 🔊22

 Betty   C

 Betty's mother   ☐

 Cousin Robert   ☐

Uncle Richard   ☐

 Betty's father   ☐

 Aunt Susan   ☐

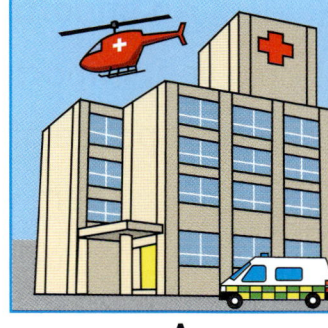

A   B

C   D

E   F

 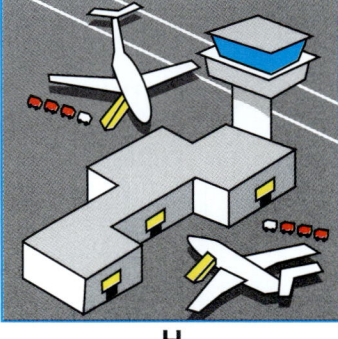

G   H

Flyers practice test

Read the text. Choose the right words and write them on the lines.

An important job

Police officers do a very important job <u>because</u> they

Example | look after us all. Most police officers are friendly people.

1 | You _____ them walking in our streets each

2 | day, or _____ driving fast cars with lights

on the top. You can watch television programmes about

3 | a police officer's job, or read about _____

work in newspapers.

The day begins very early for police officers and they

often finish work late and go to bed after midnight.

4 | They have to work _____ the weekends

and holidays too. They find out what's happening

5 | _____ in our towns and cities. Then they

go back to the office and write down information about

6 | _____ they've seen and done. They also

have meetings with other police officers.

Perhaps you'd like to be a police officer? Well you'll need

7 | _____ go to college and learn about the job.

8 | You _____ study hard, take tests and show

9 | that you _____ strong and brave. Many

people think the job is very exciting. But it's hard and it

10 | can be dangerous. Think carefully _____

you decide it's the job for you!

Flyers practice test

Example	because	when	than
1	see	saw	seeing
2	someone	something	sometimes
3	they	them	their
4	into	during	past
5	anywhere	nowhere	everywhere
6	why	what	when
7	to	by	of
8	have	must	can't
9	is	are	be
10	next	always	before

7 At the castle

Words

1 Draw lines from the words to the things in the picture.

We're going to visit a castle tomorrow with our class!

exit

flag

king

gate

ring

queen

south

postcards

bridge

swans

entrance

swings

west

river

crown

north   costumes   playground   east   steps

2 Ask and answer.

This is the exit, isn't it?

No, it isn't. It's the entrance.

Listening

1 The teacher is talking to the children in class about the school trip to the castle. Listen and write the missing information. 🔊23

Trip to castle
Important information

Day of trip: **(1)** <u>Wednesday</u>

Date: **(2)** _____ June

Name of castle: **(3)** _____ Castle

(4) _____ a.m.   leave school (early start)

Journey will take: **(5)** _____ hours

11 a.m.   Tour of castle building: **(6)** _____ and museum

(7) _____ p.m.   Lunch: remember your sandwiches and buy **(8)** _____ from castle restaurant

2 p.m.   Walk round castle gardens and see river.

Find out about **(9)** _____ animals and unusual insects like spiders and

(10) _____

(11) _____ p.m.   Arrive back at school

Please bring: camera

(12) _____

(13) _____

And money for: postcards

(14) _____ and ice creams

Have a great trip!

> Remember!
> We use 'will' and 'going to' to talk about the future.

Conversation

1 **Listen, read and act.** 🔊 24

Mr Brown is talking to Holly and Harry about their trip.

Mr Brown: Are you going to go on a trip to the castle tomorrow?

Holly and Harry: Yes, we are!

Mr Brown: What are you going to do there?

Holly: I'm going to look at the insects in the insect house!

Harry: I hate insects! I'm going to go to the playground.

Holly: Oh, Dad, we need some money because we're going to buy some postcards.

Harry: And some ice cream!

Mr Brown: Well, it's going to be cloudy tomorrow and it might rain. So make sure you take your umbrellas.

Holly: OK, we will, Dad!

Mr Brown: And are you going to do your homework before you go to bed?

Holly and Harry: No, we aren't! We're too excited!

2 **You are going to visit the castle tomorrow, but you can only visit three places. Look at the list and tick (✓). Ask and answer.**

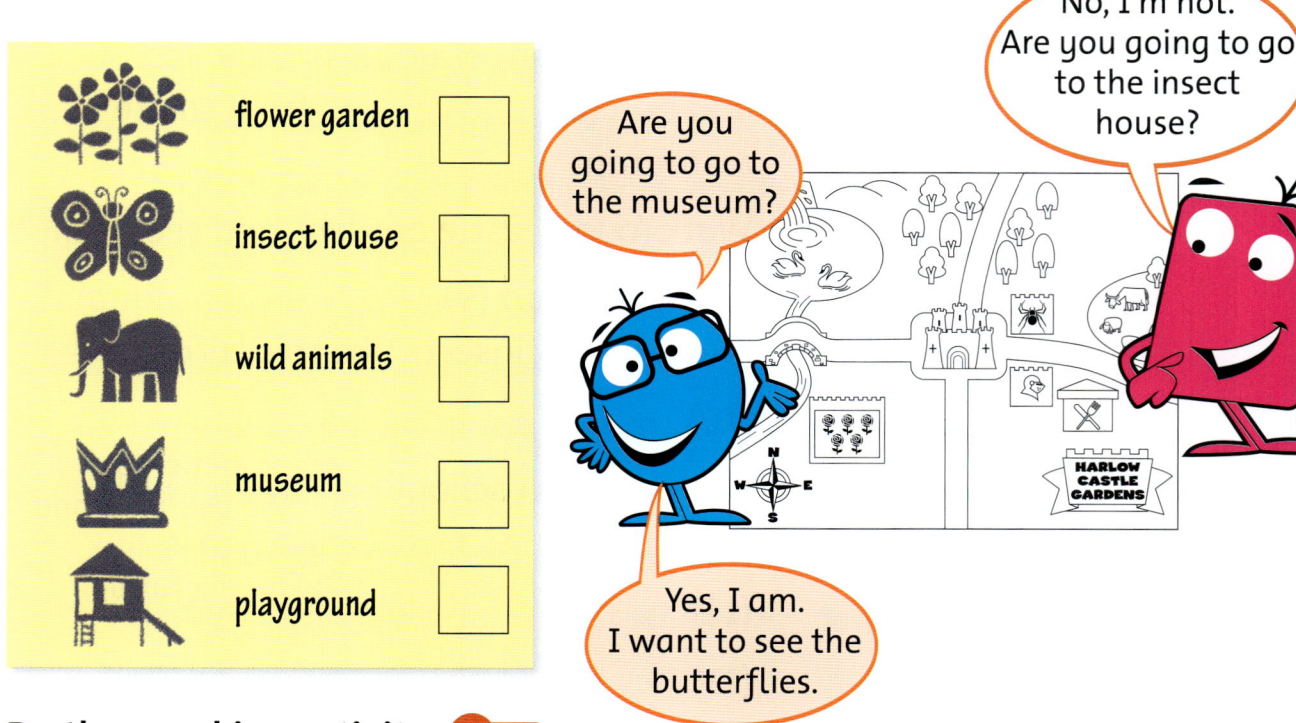

flower garden ☐

insect house ☐

wild animals ☐

museum ☐

playground ☐

Are you going to go to the museum?

No, I'm not. Are you going to go to the insect house?

Yes, I am. I want to see the butterflies.

3 **Do the speaking activity.** 🅿 135

Where's the restaurant?

Leave the castle and go east. Go past the museum and it's the next building on the right.

Reading & writing

1 It's Wednesday evening and Mrs Brown is talking to Holly and Harry. Read their conversation and write the missing words.

spent   ~~did~~   walked   do   saw   send

Mrs Brown: Did you have a good trip to the castle today, Harry?

Harry: Yes, I (**1**) _____ did _____ ! I (**2**) _____ all my money on this castle made of card.

Mrs Brown: What did you (**3**) _____ on the trip to the castle, Holly?

Holly: I (**4**) _____ all the rooms in the castle and then I (**5**)_____ through the castle gardens!

Mrs Brown: And you've got a postcard, Holly.

Holly: Yes, I'm going to (**6**) _____ it to Grandma tomorrow.

Mrs Brown: Are you going to do your homework before you go to bed?

Holly and Harry: No, we aren't! We're too excited!

2 Holly is writing about the journey to the castle and what she did when she arrived. Join the sentence halves and write the missing words.

over   high   ~~early~~   cheap   arrived   bought   left   had

1 It was very _____ early _____ in the morning

2 The bus went _____ up in the hills

3 The bus went _____ the bridge

4 The postcards were quite _____ so

a and we _____ in front of the castle.

b I _____ one for my grandma.

c when we _____ school on the bus.

d so we _____ an amazing view of the castle.

Words

1 Read the sentences and circle the words in the wordsearch puzzle.

1 Birds on the river.

2 You go into the castle here.

3 The way out.

4 Buy these at the castle shop.

5 A butterfly is a pretty one.

6 A kind of door into a garden.

7 Go over water on this.

8 You walk up these to enter.

9 You wear it on your finger.

10 You sit on this in the playground.

11 Something to eat between meals.

12 A woman who wears a crown.

13 You need this if it rains.

14 Look at this to find your way.

15 There's one on top of the castle.

16 Children dress up in these.

2 Follow the instructions, draw lines and write the letters.
Find a word which describes the trip to the castle.

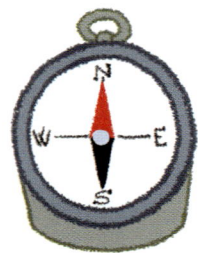

a	e	m	p	h	f	l	e	i
q	b	r	o	c	j	g	n	d
n	a	c	e	b	o	l	z	y
j	c	l	s	x	d	h	x	k
m	u	g	n	b	t	e	i	t
l	v	p	z	e	f	w	l	k

Start here

Instructions:

1 ~~east four~~   6 south two

2 north two   7 west three

3 west three   8 south two

4 north three   9 east five

5 east five

The castle trip was _e_ __ __ __ __ __ __ __ __ __ !

Extended reading: Holly's diary

1 Read Holly's diary. Do the activity on the photocopiable worksheet.

 136

24th May

Dear Diary,

Yesterday we went on a school trip to Harlow Castle. Harry and I had to get up very early in the morning – at half past six! I sat next to Katy on the bus journey and we looked at the view from the window. When we arrived at the castle a friendly man appeared and gave us a tour of the castle building.

Now I'm going to write about all the things I saw in the castle!

We couldn't go everywhere in the castle but these were the rooms we saw. First we went in some of the rooms downstairs. We walked into the **'Great Hall'** and there on the walls we saw paintings of all the old kings and queens. There was a really long table and on it were lots of beautiful plates and silver knives and forks. The **kitchen** was enormous, and on the shelves there were very old bowls and glass bottles from the seventeenth century! Can you believe that? Well, then we went to the **living room**. It was really interesting. The Queens' gold rings, bracelets and necklaces were on a table there but we couldn't actually touch them. After that we went into the **library**. There we saw bookcases with lots of books on them and letters from the old kings and queens. I enjoyed reading them because I'm interested in history. Then we went upstairs. I really liked the **Queen's bedroom**. On a shelf near her bed were beautiful combs with designs of strange creatures on them. The **King's bedroom** was darker and had a very large wooden desk in it. I thought it was ugly!
And in the **bathroom** there was the biggest mirror in the world! I was really pleased we went on that trip!

2 Holly is talking to her mum about what she did in the castle gardens. Listen and do the photocopiable activity. 25 136

Flyers practice test

Read the text. Choose the right words and write them on the lines.

Windsor Castle

Example The largest and __most__ famous castle in England is called Windsor Castle. Kings and Queens have often lived there. A special

1 flag flies from the top of the castle _____ the King or Queen is at home.

2 In the 13th century King Henry the third built the large apartments in the castle. You can still go inside the castle, _____ a tour of these apartments and learn about English history.

3 _____ you like to visit Windsor Castle? The best time

4 to go is in the autumn _____ there's a big festival at that time of year, and Windsor is very busy during the summer.

Queen Mary's Dolls' House

5 In Windsor Castle you can see _____ very unusual and lovely. Queen Mary's Dolls' House is a very old toy house.

6 When you look _____ the front door you can see a hall with paintings on the walls by real artists. The lights come on and go off in all the rooms. In the library, bookcases are full of

7 books that you can read. Stairs go _____ to the bedrooms

8 _____ dolls have cupboards full of the most amazing

9 clothes, brushes and combs. You really _____ see it!

10 To find _____ more about Windsor Castle and Queen Mary's Dolls' House visit this website: www.royalcollection.org.uk

Flyers practice test

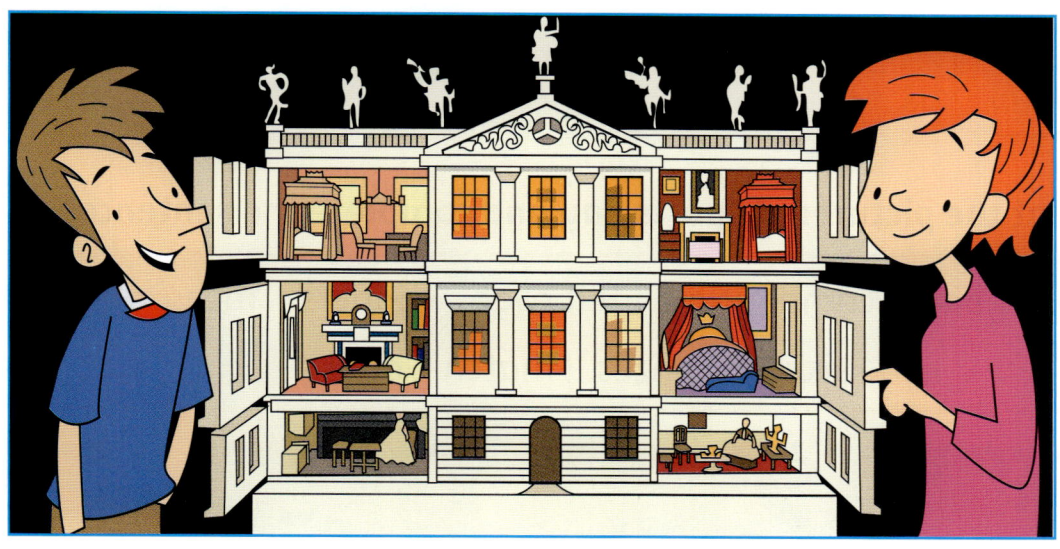

Example	most	much	many
1	who	when	what
2	has	have	had
3	Could	Should	Would
4	so	than	because
5	something	everything	anything
6	between	through	down
7	up	by	at
8	which	whose	where
9	need	must	can't
10	out	off	over

8 Sports day!

Words

1 Look at the pictures of sports day and complete the sentences.

> ~~volleyball~~ competition fell over winners race golf
> scored prizes match goal

A great game of
___volleyball___!

Harry _____
during the
running _____.

The children
had an
exciting _____!

Harry _____
an excellent
_____.

Everyone enjoyed
playing _____.

The high jump
_____.

The _____!

The _____!

2 Match the sentences to the words.

1 A team game.

2 A game you can play with another person.

3 A place where people watch sport.

4 You need to know this to find out who's winning.

5 The winner gets this.

6 When people run to find out who's the fastest.

tennis

volleyball

the prize

a race

a stadium

the score

Listening & reading

1 Listen to Holly explaining what's going to happen at her school sports day. Write a tick (✓) or a cross (✗) next to the pictures. Then write 'm' for morning or 'a' for afternoon. 🔊26

2 Draw lines to match the question tags to the correct sentences.

isn't it?   aren't we?   are we?   can we?

1 It's going to be a great day, _____?

2 We can't see all the competitions, _____?

3 We're going to have a good time, _____?

4 We aren't very good at running, Katy, _____?

5 George and Harry are going to run fast, _____?

6 Harry doesn't run very fast, _____?

7 You play volleyball well, Holly, _____?

8 It isn't very sunny today, _____?

is it?   does he?   don't you?   aren't they?

GRAMMAR Tag questions page 119

Conversation

1 Listen and read. Then act. 🔊 27

Mrs Brown: Hello, Holly. So who do you think is going to win the 200-metre race?

Holly: The race has finished! George has already won!

Mrs Brown: Oh dear! Never mind! Did you see the volleyball match?

Holly: It hasn't started yet. It starts at three o'clock.

Mrs Brown: Oh good! What time's the football match?

Holly: The football match has just started, Mum!

Mrs Brown: Oh no!

Holly: Well, you're very late!

Mrs Brown: I know ... I'm sorry. I couldn't find my house key.

Holly: Oh no, not again, Mum!

Mrs Brown: Yes, and now I've lost my car key!

Look! Use 'already' for something that has happened or been done.

2 Make sentences. Match them with the pictures.

1 has / Mrs Brown / the school / just / at / arrived /

   <u>Mrs Brown has just arrived at the school.</u> — f

2 made / cakes / The parents / already / snacks / and / have

   _____ □

3 just / The teachers / tidied / the classrooms / have

   _____ □

4 flags / the playground / put / already / in / have / The children

   _____ □

5 have / their tickets / paid / The parents / already / for

   _____ □

6 prizes / hasn't / The sports teacher / yet / the children / their / given

   _____ □

 a    b    c    d    e    f

GRAMMAR Present perfect, *yet* page 119

Listening

1 Listen to the teacher. He's talking to the children and parents about sports day. Write the missing information. 🔊 28

21ST JUNE PRIZE WINNERS!

200-metre race	**Example**
winner:	George
prize for being (**1**) _____ :	Harry

Football match	
first half score:	2 / 1
score at end of match:	(**2**) _____
winning team:	the (**3**) _____

Volleyball match	
score at end of match:	(**4**) _____
winning team:	the (**5**) _____

Money!

Money from sports day is for the school camping (**6**) _____

2 Now make sentences about sports day.

Katy	has	made	an amazing day.
Harry	have	won	the 200-metre race.
The school		heard	some delicious cakes and snacks.
We		seen	very brave.
George		had	some great matches.
I		eaten	the high jump competition.
		been	over £300.

Writing & speaking

1 **Katy has written about the 200-metre race for the school magazine. Write the missing words in the sentences. Then number the pictures in the correct order.**

> hurt ~~went~~ smiled waved ~~waited~~ gave held won fell
> began ran came

1 The boys and girls ___went___ to the starting line and ___waited___ for the race to begin.

2 The sports teacher _____ her flag and the race _____.

3 During the race, Harry _____ and _____ himself but he was very brave.

4 George _____ across the finishing line first and _____ the race.

5 The teacher _____ George a prize because he _____ first in the race.

6 George _____ up the silver cup and _____ at his parents.

 1

2 **Do the speaking activity.** P 137

There's a football match.

Flyers practice test

Listen and draw lines. There is one example. 🔊29

Daisy   Michael   Fred   Mary

Richard   Jim   Sally

Flyers practice test

Look at the picture and read the story. Write some words to complete the sentences about the story. You can use 1, 2, 3 or 4 words.

Sports day at school

Hello! I'm Holly and Harry's Mum and I had a very busy morning! It was sports day at the children's school. My other daughter, Emma, is only three so she hasn't started school yet. I decided to take her with me to see the older children doing their sports. We were leaving the house when Emma remembered her new doll. She wanted to take it with her and she was crying. I went into Emma's bedroom. It was really untidy! I found the doll under a blanket. Emma smiled happily when I gave it to her.

We were ready to go. I looked for my keys but I couldn't find them anywhere. Then Emma pointed at the sofa in the living room and there they were under a cushion. I don't know how they got there. We left the house and walked to the school quickly. When we arrived, we saw my daughter, Holly. She didn't say 'hello' to us and she was a bit unfriendly, actually. She told me I was really late.

I missed the children's race, but Harry told me he fell over in it and hurt his knee. When I saw him, he had a bandage on it. He said it was very sore, but he was actually OK. During the volleyball match a dog went onto the field and ran away with the ball! All the children were trying to catch the dog! The dog was very excited and thought it was a wonderful game. Round and round the children ran! The sports teacher looked very unhappy about it! 'Whose dog is that?' he shouted angrily! And he didn't talk about the dog when he gave the children their prizes! But I thought it was a wonderful day! Holly plays for a team called the Sharks and they won, so she was happy too in the end.

Flyers practice test

Examples

Betty Brown was very ____busy____ this morning.

At her children's school it was _sports day_ .

Questions

1 Betty's daughter, Emma _____ school yet.

2 Emma wanted to take her _____ to the school.

3 Betty found what Emma wanted _____ in the bedroom.

4 Betty's keys were in the living room under a _____.

5 Holly wasn't happy with her mum because her mum got to school very _____.

6 Harry told his mum that his _____ was very sore.

7 Betty had a wonderful _____.

Revision 2

1 Look at the pictures. Write the names of the jobs in the boxes.

1. `a` `c` `t` `o` `r`
2. ☐☐☐☐☐☐
3. ☐☐☐☐☐☐☐☐☐
4. ☐☐☐☐☐☐☐
5. ☐☐☐☐☐☐☐☐☐
6. ☐☐☐☐☐☐☐

2 Draw lines to two balloons to find the words that start with 'ex'.
Read the sentences and write. Then colour.

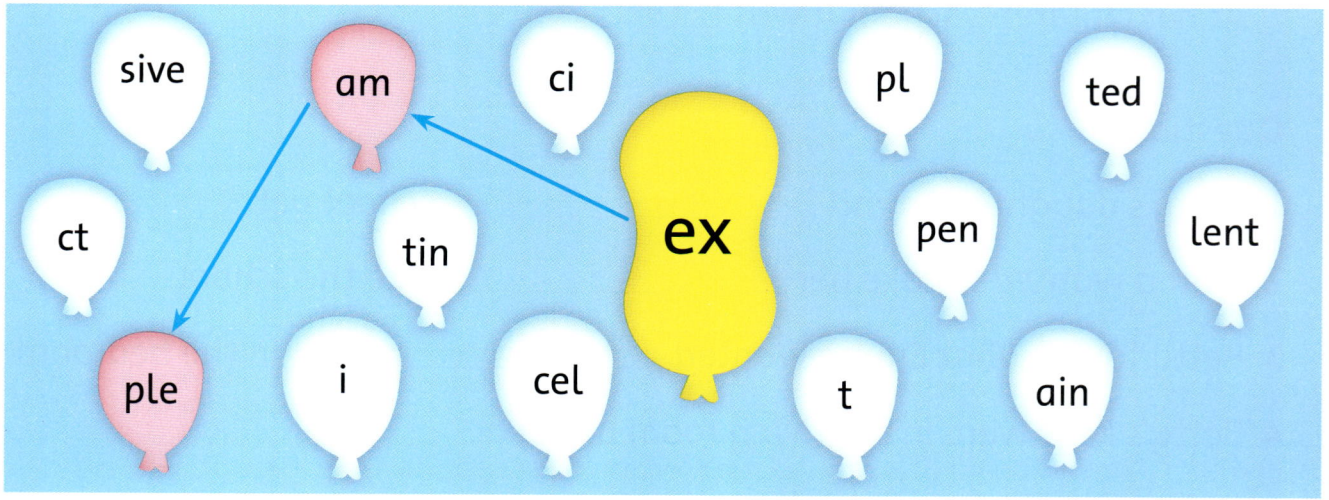

1   This is the one that shows you what to do. _example_ (pink)

2   Dinosaurs are now_____. (orange)

3   You leave a building here. _____ (red)

4   Really, really good work! _____! (purple)

5   You feel like this before you go on a trip. _____ (brown)

6   Not cheap. _____ (green)

7   If you don't understand your teacher will do this. _____ (grey)

3 Match the pictures with the sentences and add the question tag.

    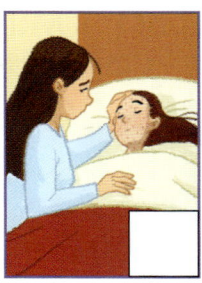 

1 Tony's very good at football, _____*isn't he*_____?

2 You're late again, _____?

3 You aren't very well, _____?

4 Your bedroom isn't very tidy, _____?

5 Helen looks very pretty, _____?

6 I can read well, _____?

are you?

~~isn't he?~~

can't I?

doesn't she?

is it?

aren't you?

4 Read the story and write the missing words.

~~saw~~ was drive go went fly were
flying driving invented flew living

Hello. My name's Tony. Last week I (**1**) _____*saw*_____ a really great film when I (**2**) _____ to the cinema. It was about a kind man who lived in an unusual house with his two children. They (**3**) _____ very poor but the man (**4**) _____ an engineer and he (**5**) _____ lots of exciting things for them. One day he bought a really old car, which used to be a racing car. The engine didn't work and there were no tyres on the wheels. He worked hard to repair it and make it special. When it was ready he decided to (**6**) _____ the car to a beach for a picnic. He took his children with him and they were (**7**) _____ up a road though the hills when the car suddenly (**8**) _____ into the air. It had large wings and it could (**9**) _____! The children couldn't believe it! They were (**10**) _____ like birds, high up in the sky! After a few hours they arrived at a strange castle. A very unkind man was (**11**) _____ in the castle and he tried to take their car. If you want to know what happened next, you'll have to (**12**) _____ and see the film.

REVISION 2 WORDS   page 116

5 **Listen to the conversation and look at the pictures. Who does each thing, Bill or his Mum? Draw lines.** 🔊30

6 **What have you done today? Write sentences.**

I've already _____

and I've _____

but I haven't _____

and I haven't _____ yet.

1 Write about a day out. Then ask and answer with a friend.

2 Find ten more differences. Talk to your friend about the pictures.

3 Use these words and talk about what you did last weekend and what you're going to do next weekend.

> play / played   watch / watched   visit / visited
>
> go / went   see / saw   eat / ate

4 Now do the Speaking test. **P** 124–125

9 Our camping adventure

Words

1 Harry and Holly are on the school camping trip. Find things in the picture and draw lines.

stars   swan   cave   bats

rucksack   river

tent   rocks

magazine   nest

moon   hills

newspaper   wing

torch   bridge

fire   umbrella   biscuits   pockets

Speaking & words

1 **Do the speaking activity.**  138

Mum, are Harry and Holly there yet?

Yes, it's half past six now. They arrived three hours ago.

2 **Look at the pictures and the letters. Write the words.**

1  r e h g t t e o

together

2  e y v a h

3  e e d p

4  o l e a n

5 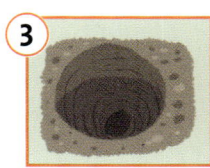 y r f u r

6 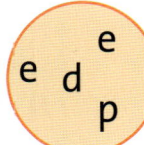 l g e a r

7  d r a k

8  g e r s n t a

9  f e h n g t r i e d

10  r i b o h l e

3 **Write the words from Activity 2 in these sentences.**

1 The hole at the entrance to the cave was very _____deep_____.

2 We saw a very _____ cave in the forest. It was really big!

3 That's a _____ creature! It's got three eyes.

4 Holly and Harry went on their adventure _____.

5 Come and touch this rabbit. It's really soft and _____.

6 The rucksack was very _____!

7 You shouldn't walk in the forest _____.

8 Holly was _____ when she suddenly saw a bat.

9 I hate bats! They've got big wings and they're _____!

10 The cave was very _____ inside.

Reading & writing

1 This is the story of the start of Holly and Harry's adventure. Write the missing words.

put   ~~whispered~~   arrived   hurt   decided   walked

Harry (**1**) _whispered_ 'Let's have an adventure!' He (**2**) _____ several snacks in his pockets. We (**3**) _____ straight on up the path by the river. On the way, Harry (**4**) _____ himself on a rock. We (**5**) _____ at the entrance to a cave. We (**6**) _____ to go in.

2 Match the sentences with the pictures.

a The other children were telling stories... [1]

b We were walking through the woods... [ ]

c Harry was whistling a happy tune... [ ]

d We were feeling a bit frightened... [ ]

e The teachers were reading newspapers and magazines... [ ]

f The silver moon and stars were shining... [ ]

These sentences paint a picture of the story and make it more interesting.

GRAMMAR   **Past continuous** page 119

Listening & writing

1 **Holly is writing about the adventure she had with Harry. Put the missing sentences from page 78 into her story.**

22nd July

Harry and I were a bit bored. While (1) [a] near the camp fire, Harry whispered to me 'I'm going to go and explore!' 'You can't go by yourself,' I said. 'I'm coming with you.'

He went to his tent and put several snacks in his pockets. I put some blankets and sweaters in a rucksack but Harry said it was too heavy and we couldn't take it with us. (2) ☐ when we left our tents so we could see well. We didn't need to use the torch.

We walked, as quietly as we could, past the swans and the little bridge and then straight on up the path by the river. (3) ☐ by the fire so they didn't see us.

We could see a wonderful view of the hills. (4) ☐ but I told him to stop because it was too noisy. While (5) ☐, Harry fell over and hurt his toe. It was sore, but he was very brave.

It was very late in the evening when suddenly we saw a hole between the rocks. It was the entrance to a cave. 'We shouted 'Hello!' but no-one was there. (6) ☐ but we decided to go in.

2 **The teacher is phoning Mrs Brown, who is writing down some information for her husband. Listen and write the missing words.** 🔊31

Richard,

Holly and Harry were missing from the camping trip last night!

They went to visit a cave (1) _____two_____ kilometres from where they were camping! They were alone all night!

Now they're at the (2) _____ in town.

Harry has a broken (3) _____ and Holly has hurt her (4) _____.

Visiting hours this evening are between six o'clock and half past eight.

Ask for the (5) _____ room and speak to Nurse (6) _____.

They had something to eat for lunch: (7) _____ and chips.
Come soon!

Betty

Words

1 Look at the pictures in the first grid. Write the first letter of each word in the second grid to complete the crossword.

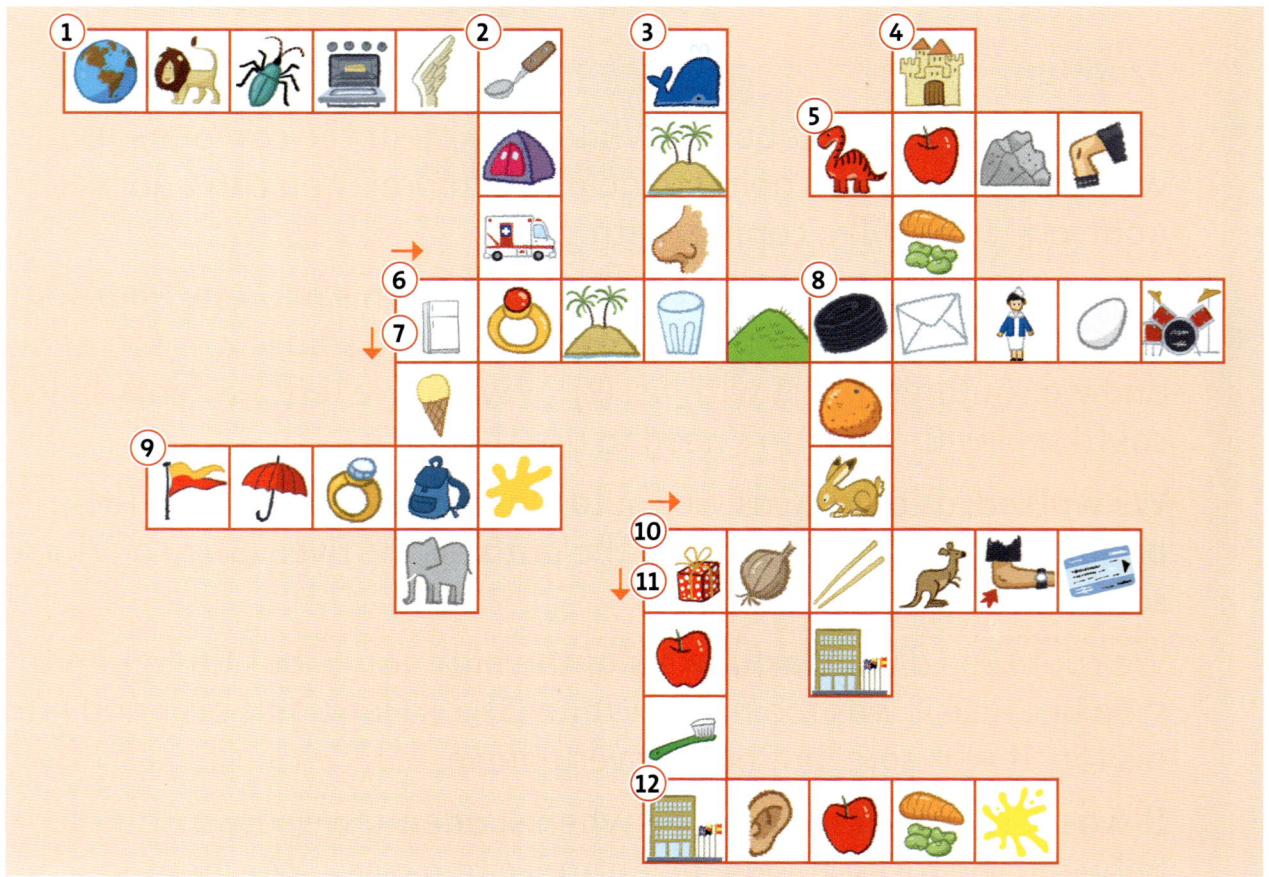

UNIT 9
WORDS   page 116

Extended reading: Holly's diary

1 **Read Holly's diary. Order the pictures.**

22nd July

Dear Diary,

I'm going to write about what happened on our adventure!

Harry and I saw a hole in the rocks and we decided to go inside and explore. It was a deep cave and on the wall there were paintings of dinosaurs and other extinct creatures that have disappeared from our planet. It was amazing! It looked like something from our history books at school. Suddenly I saw something strange. A bat! Bats **(1)** were living in the cave! And there were hundreds of insects! Then something soft **(2)** _____ up my arm. It was an enormous spider! It was as big as my hand! It was horrible.

Suddenly, everything went dark. Harry's torch **(3)** _____! We couldn't see anything. We were alone and that was really frightening.

We stayed together and tried to find our way back to the entrance of the cave. In the end we found it. Harry looked at his watch. It was just after midnight. Then, suddenly, we heard a loud noise. It was a storm! Soon it **(4)** _____ hard. We decided to go back inside. While we were making a fire to keep warm, I burned my finger. I **(5)** _____ but Harry was very brave. He remembered he had biscuits and chocolate in his pockets. We ate all the food and I felt a bit better then. We lay down and spent the night there. During the night we could hear strange noises.

The next morning we had a big surprise when we woke up. We heard the sound of children outside the cave. They **(6)** _____ our names. All our friends were there and our teacher too.

Mum and Dad are still very angry with us and say we can never go camping again. We're really unhappy about that.

2 **Write the missing words.**

> wasn't working   was crying   were shouting
> ~~were living~~   was raining   was walking

Flyers practice test

Vicky is talking to her friend, Mary. What does Mary say? Read the conversation and choose the best answer. Write a letter (A–H) for each answer. You do not need to use all the letters.

Example:

Vicky:	What are you doing this weekend?
Mary:	B

Questions

1 Vicky: Where are you going to stay?

Mary: _____

2 Vicky: Lucky you! Do you like camping?

Mary: _____

3 Vicky: I'm going to the cinema this weekend. What type of films do you like?

Mary: _____

4 Vicky: Well, do you want to go and see a good film with me when you get back?

Mary: _____

5 Vicky: Great! Have a wonderful weekend. Are you excited?

Mary: _____

A Yes, I am! Have a good weekend, too.

B I'm going on a camping trip! **(Example)**

C I don't really like that film.

D I like adventure films.

E Thanks. I'd really like to do that!

F In large tents up in the hills.

G Why do you want to go there there?

H Yes, I do. it's fun!

Flyers practice test

Listen and colour and write. There is one example. 🔊32

10 A good year!

Words

1 Write letters to match to the pictures. Write the words in the sentences.

Here are some of the things that we do at different times of the year.

What do you like to do at different times of the year?

playing going riding buying walking
collecting flying lying eating growing skiing
snowboarding making throwing ~~climbing~~

a

h

1 ___climbing___ up hills [m]

2 _____ in the garden [ ]

b

i

3 _____ snowballs [ ]

4 _____ tennis [ ]

c

5 _____ on a boat trip [ ]

j

6 _____ on sledges [ ]

k

d

7 _____ new clothes [ ]

8 _____ in the woods [ ]

l

e

9 _____ leaves [ ]

m

10 _____ down the hill [ ]

f

11 _____ kites [ ]

n

12 _____ on the beach [ ]

13 _____ a snowman [ ]

g

o

14 _____ vegetables [ ]

15 _____ down mountains [ ]

Words & listening

1 Look at the pictures on page 84. When in the year are Holly and Harry doing these things? Write.

Spring

_____

_____

_____

Summer

_____

_____

_____

Autumn

_____

_____

_____

Winter

snowboarding, throwing snowballs

_____

2 Frank and Sophia, two children in Holly's class at school, are talking about the things they like doing in the winter. Listen and number the pictures. 🔊 33

a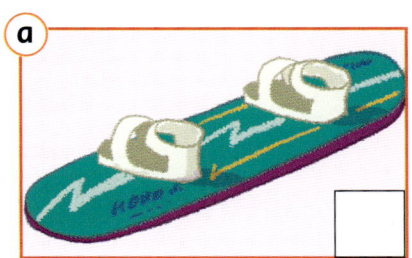

b  1

c

d

e

f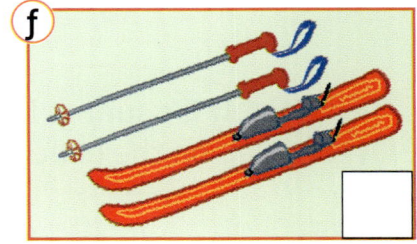

3 Can you remember who liked these things?
Talk with a friend. Listen again.

Conversation

1 Listen and read. Then act. 🔊 34

George: It's raining! What shall we do?

Katy: Shall we play a board game?

George: That's a good idea. What do you do if the weather's nice, Katy?

Katy: Well, if it's sunny I lie down by the swimming pool and read my book.

George: I go swimming in the pool if it's sunny. You're very lazy!

Katy: No, I'm not! What do you do if the sky's grey and if it's foggy and cold?

George: If it's foggy and cold, I put on my sweater, my coat and my scarf and I go for a walk in the woods.

Katy: If the weather's foggy and cold, I stay inside and watch cartoons on the children's channel! What do you do if it's snowing, George?

George: If it's snowing I make a large snowman in the garden.

Katy: Oh, I don't! I stay in bed!

George: You really are very lazy!

Katy: Perhaps I am! But if there's a storm, I watch the sky from the window.

George: Oh, if there's a storm, I hide under the bed!

Katy: So you aren't very brave, George!

George: No, I'm really not!

2 Talk to your friends about the weather.

What do you do if ...

- there's a storm?
- it's sunny?
- it's snowing?
- it's foggy?
- it's raining?

> Remember! We use the present simple after *if*.

3 Work with a friend. Match the pictures and order the instructions. P 139

> If it's sunny, I lie on the beach.

GRAMMAR *If clauses* page 119

Listening

1 The teacher is having a conversation with Harry. Listen to the conversation. Who talks about these things? Listen and draw lines. 🔊35

Reading & writing

Harry has written about what he did last year.

1 Colour round the pictures to match them with the writing boxes.

I visited an amazing castle in _____ After we went round the castle, I went to the insect house with my friend, Oliver. We saw butterflies and beetles there. While we _____ at them, a spider dropped onto Oliver's head. He was really frightened!

In _____January_____ William entered the chess competition at school. He __was playing__ for over two hours and he was the winner. I was so pleased with him.

1

I've been at school for four months and it's _____ now. Yesterday I had a snowball fight with my brother and sisters. While we _____ snowballs, Emma started to cry because a hard snowball hit her elbow and it was really sore. She's OK now though.

In _____ Holly and I went on a camping trip and stayed in tents. One night we went to explore and found a cave. While we _____ in the cave trying to sleep, we heard strange noises. I'm sure there were frightening creatures in that cave!

In _____ I went to the circus. I loved the clowns. The best clown _____ a really unusual bike. It only had one wheel and one tyre!

In _____ we all went to a restaurant because it was it was Grandma's 80th birthday. Everyone said the pizzas were delicious and Grandma _____ when the waiter brought the cake to our table.

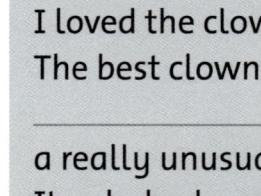

2 Write the missing words on the pages. Look back at Holly's diary pages to help you write the months.

> April   July   December   May   ~~January~~   March

> ~~was playing~~   were throwing   was smiling
> were looking   was riding   were lying

3 Number the different things Harry did in the correct order.

Flyers practice test

Listen and write. There is one example. 🔊 36

MUSEUM INFORMATION

	Name of museum:	<u>Laketown</u> Science Museum
1	Closes on:	_____ December
2	Opening hours:	9 a.m. – _____ p.m.
3	Best time to visit:	in the _____
4	Interesting things for children:	History of the telephone and of _____
5	Address:	_____ Green _____ Road

Flyers practice test

Read the text. Choose the right words and write them on the lines.

The Great Pyramid of Giza

Example   There are __over__ a hundred pyramids in Egypt. The most famous is the Great Pyramid of Giza. This pyramid is over 4,500

1 years old. _____ the early 19th century it was

2 actually the _____ building on Earth! It stands next to the River Nile near the city of Cairo in Egypt. It is over

3 140 metres high and it _____ the Egyptian people

4 twenty years to build. There are _____ than two million pieces of stone in the pyramid . You can still see a large

5 and unusual kind of animal _____ this pyramid.

6 It is called 'The Sphinx' and it _____ the body of a lion and the head of an Egyptian king.

7 You can learn a lot about Egyptian history _____

8 you look at the walls of the pyramid. _____ these walls are paintings of people and animals. The paintings show

9 _____ people lived in Egypt at that time.

You can go inside the pyramid but you have to buy a ticket. They sell 300 tickets each day, 150 in the morning at 8 a.m. and 150 in the afternoon at 1 p.m. You can't take photographs inside the pyramid.

10 If you _____ in Egypt you really must go and see the Great Pyramid of Giza!

Flyers practice test

Example	over	into	past
1	Across	Until	Below
2	tall	taller	tallest
3	take	took	taken
4	much	many	more
5	through	near	into
6	has	have	had
7	or	so	if
8	On	Up	To
9	when	how	who
10	be	is	are

11 Our summer holidays

Words

1 Look at the pictures and the letters. Write the words.

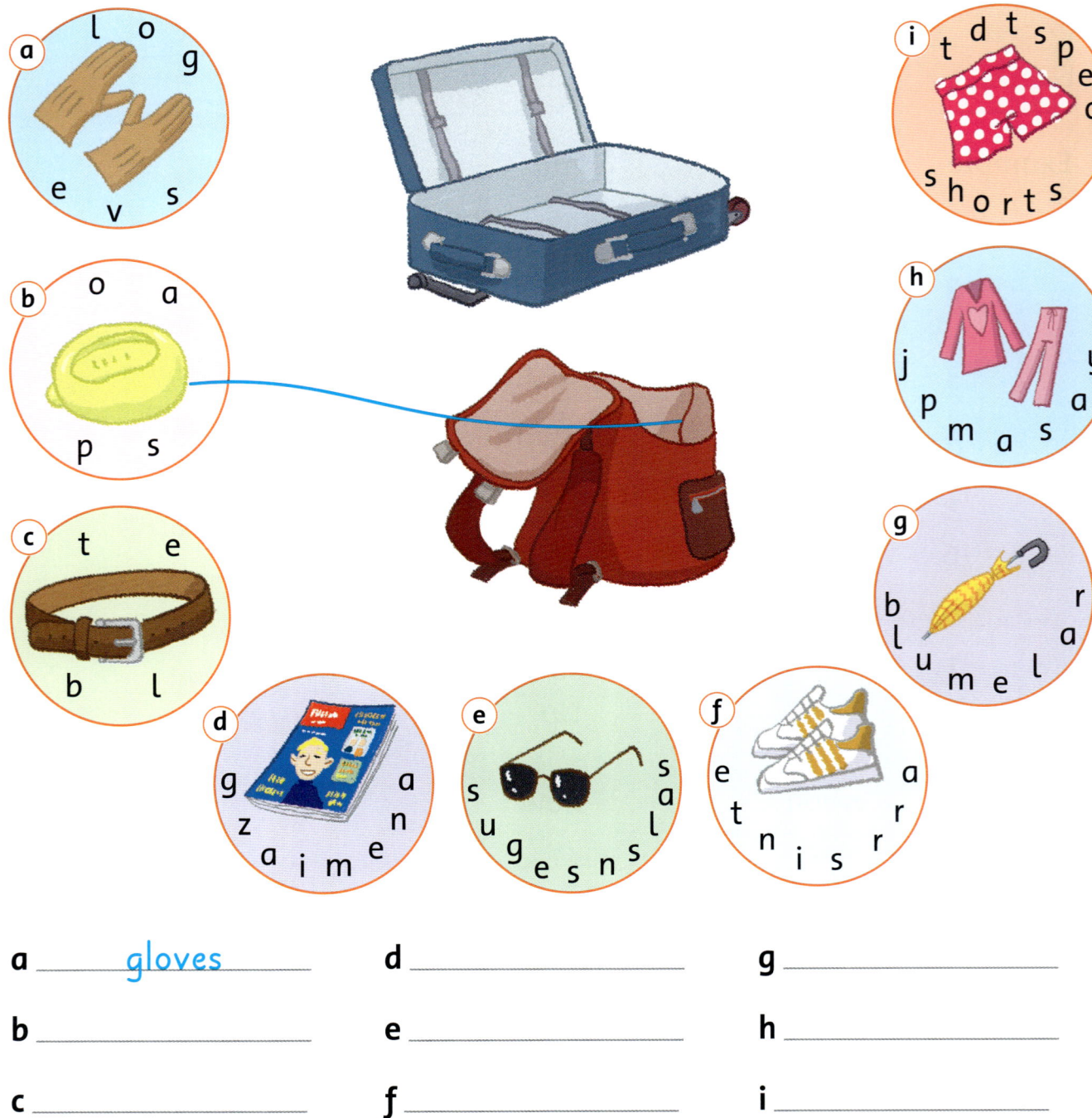

a ___gloves___   d _____   g _____

b _____   e _____   h _____

c _____   f _____   i _____

2 The Brown family are getting ready for their holiday. Listen to their conversation and draw lines to the rucksack or the suitcase. 🔊37

What clothes don't go in the rucksack or the suitcase?

_____

UNIT 11 WORDS   page 117

Story

1 Listen and read. Then act.

2 What should you take on these holidays? Write two things. Then talk about it with a friend.

- A skiing holiday _____ _____
- A camping holiday _____ _____
- A beach holiday _____ _____

3 Do the speaking activity. **P** 140

Reading & speaking

1 Harry is talking about what happened at the start of their holiday. In groups of three, read a part of the story. Then talk about the story together and decide which part of the story comes first, second and third. **P** 141

a

b

c

2 Katy and Sue are having a conversation. Read and make sentences.

Where's Holly today?

Have you ever flown on a plane?

She's going to see the pyramids! Have you ever seen the pyramids?

And she's going to ride a camel. Have you ever ridden a camel?

She's gone to Egypt on a plane!

No, I haven't! Planes are bad for the environment so we always travel by train.

No, I haven't.

Yes I have. But not in Egypt, I was at the zoo.

Holly's going to	fly	on a camel	.
	seen		
Have you ever	ride	the pyramids	?
	flown	on a plane	
	see		
	ridden		

Writing & speaking

1 **Write the words under the pictures.**

> an octopus   a tent   a mountain   a competition
> a helicopter   baseball   ~~chopsticks~~   a finger

1 chopsticks   2 _____   3 _____   4 _____

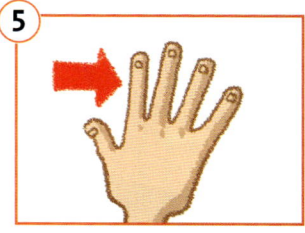   

5 _____   6 _____   7 _____   8 _____

2 **Write the past participles in the boxes.**

> ~~eaten~~   ~~climbed~~   flown   designed   burned   won   seen   stayed

Regular	Irregular
climbed	eaten

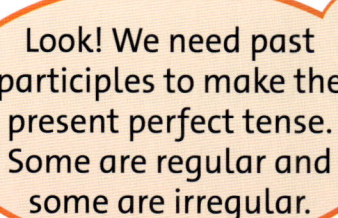

Look! We need past participles to make the present perfect tense. Some are regular and some are irregular.

3 **Have a conversation. Use the words and pictures from Activities 1 and 2.**

Have you ever eaten with chopsticks?

Yes, I have.

No, I haven't.

GRAMMAR   Irregular verbs page 120

Listening & writing

1 Holly and her mum are at the hotel. They're having a conversation. What has happened to Harry and George? Listen and draw lines. 🔊39

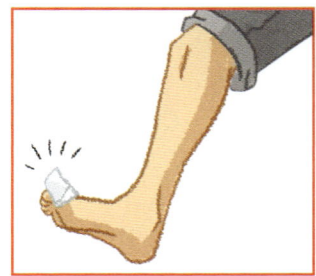
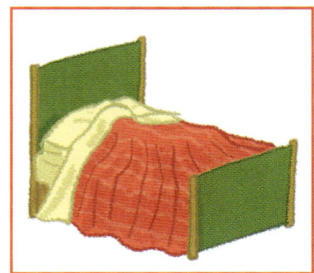

2 Write sentences about the children.

1 camels / The / on / children / ridden / have

<u>The children have ridden on camels.</u>

2 too / cakes / Harry / many / has / eaten

_____

3 medicine / doctor / The / given / some / has / Harry

_____

4 has / himself / George / too / hurt

_____

5 broken / has / toe / George / his

_____

6 has / excellent / Egypt / holiday / Holly / in / had / an

_____

Extended reading: Holly's diary

1 Read Holly's diary. Write the nouns in the **red** boxes and the verbs in the **green** and **purple** boxes.

> stairs waiter pool bed restaurant cakes head bus

> ~~was~~ pulled arrived stayed had met brought

> was crying was hurting was riding were staying

5th August

Dear Diary,

This **was** the best day of my school holidays. We _____ at a large hotel near the sea in Egypt with another family. The two dads said they wanted to see the country. The mums were very lazy and decided to lie in the sun by the _____ at the hotel and Emma _____ with them. So the two dads, and all the children, including me went off to explore. We left on a _____ very early and started our journey into the desert. We _____ at the pyramids at midday. It was hot and sunny and the air was very warm. We went on a tour inside the great pyramid. We had to climb lots of _____ in the dark. I thought it was very exciting!

Near the pyramids we _____ a very friendly man who chatted to us. He had eight camels so we all went on a camel ride. I was a bit frightened and held onto its _____ so I didn't fall. Then, my camel wouldn't move! The man _____ it and pushed it and then it started to walk, very slowly. George _____ his camel very fast when suddenly he fell off. The man helped George but George couldn't stand because his foot _____. George _____. His foot was very sore, so Dad had to carry him back to the bus.

After the camel ride we were hungry so we went to a _____ and we _____ a delicious meal there. The _____ was kind and _____ us lots of Egyptian food. Harry ate so many _____ there! Then it was time to go back. Harry felt really ill on the journey home and when we got back to the hotel he went straight to _____! I didn't! Mum took Emma and I to see some Egyptian dancers. That was a great surprise!

Flyers practice test

Listen and tick (✓) the box. There is one example. 🔊40

Where did Katy go for her summer holidays?

A  B  C

1 What time did Katy get up to travel to the airport?

A  B 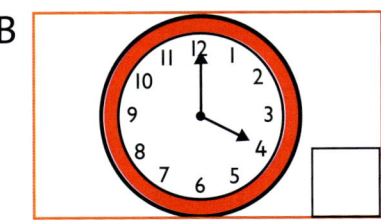 C

2 What did Katy see from the window of the plane?

A  B  C

3 Where did Katy stay when she was on holiday?

A  B  C

4 What did Katy enjoy most about her holiday?

A  B  C

Flyers practice test

Read the postcard and write the missing words. Write one word on each line.

7th August

Dear Katy,

Example   I <u>am</u> having a really great time in Egypt at the moment! The environment here is very different from in England — it's very hot and dry all the time and the sea is lovely and warm. I've seen lots of camels here! This morning we

1   all went to a beach and swam with dolphins. It _____ wonderful! Then in the afternoon we went into the desert

2   and saw some people who _____ living in tents there. I bought a really pretty bracelet for you there.

3   _____ you like the stamp on this postcard? It shows a

4   picture of the great pyramid. I went there two days _____!

5   What _____ you doing in London now? I miss you but I'll see you soon and we can go to the summer music festival together. There's different music there — pop and rock!

Lots of love

Holly

12 Past and future

Words

1 Draw lines to match the things to the places.

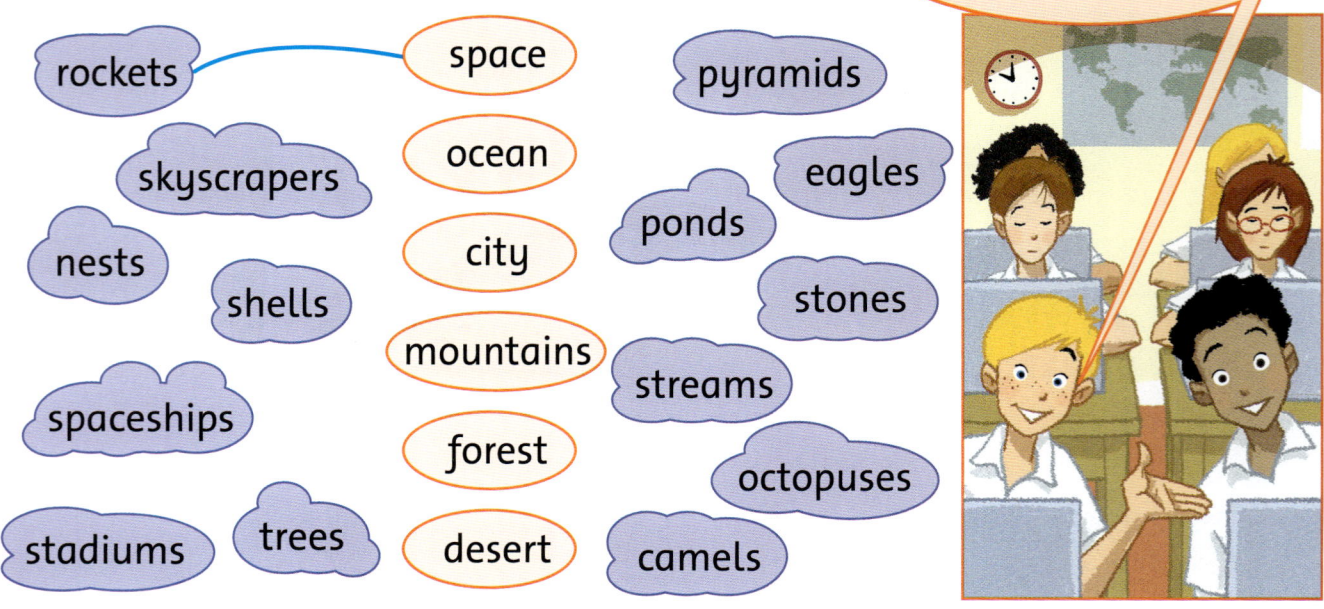

> This is our first week at our new school! We've already met our teacher and we're having a geography lesson this morning.

rockets — space

skyscrapers   ocean   pyramids

nests   city   eagles

shells   ponds

mountains   stones

spaceships   streams

forest   octopuses

stadiums   trees   desert   camels

2 Number the sentences to find out what some people believe.

> Our teacher is teaching us some interesting information, isn't she?

> Yes, she is. About a time when dinosaurs lived on our planet.

Why did dinosaurs become extinct?

a The light from the sun couldn't get to our planet, Earth. [ ]

b Plants didn't grow on the land any more. [ ]

c A large rock from another planet hit our world. [1]

d That's why dinosaurs became extinct. [ ]

e Dinosaurs had nothing to eat. [ ]

f The environment suddenly changed – the air was full of grey clouds. [ ]

Reading

1 **Draw lines to match the sentences with the pictures.**

This afternoon we're in our history lesson. We've learnt a lot about the history of London today, haven't we?

Yes, we have. We've learnt that in the 14th century, London was quite a small city.

1 People first bought newspapers in London.

2 People enjoyed watching actors on the stage at London's first theatre.

3 London had its biggest fire ever. It was called 'The Great Fire of London'. It was very frightening.

4 There were walls all round the city to make it safe. It looked like a really large castle!

5 People saw fire fighters and fire engines on the streets of London for the first time.

6 People flew from the first airport in the world. It was in a part of south London called Croydon.

a

b

c

d

e

f

2 **Look at Activity 1. When did these things happen? Guess and write.**

15th century ☐

16th century ☐

17th century ☐

18th century ☐

19th century ☐

20th century ☐

Remember! A century is one hundred years.

Writing

1 **Write the missing words.**

Now, we're learning about the 19th century.

We're finding out what it was like to live in England two hundred years ago!

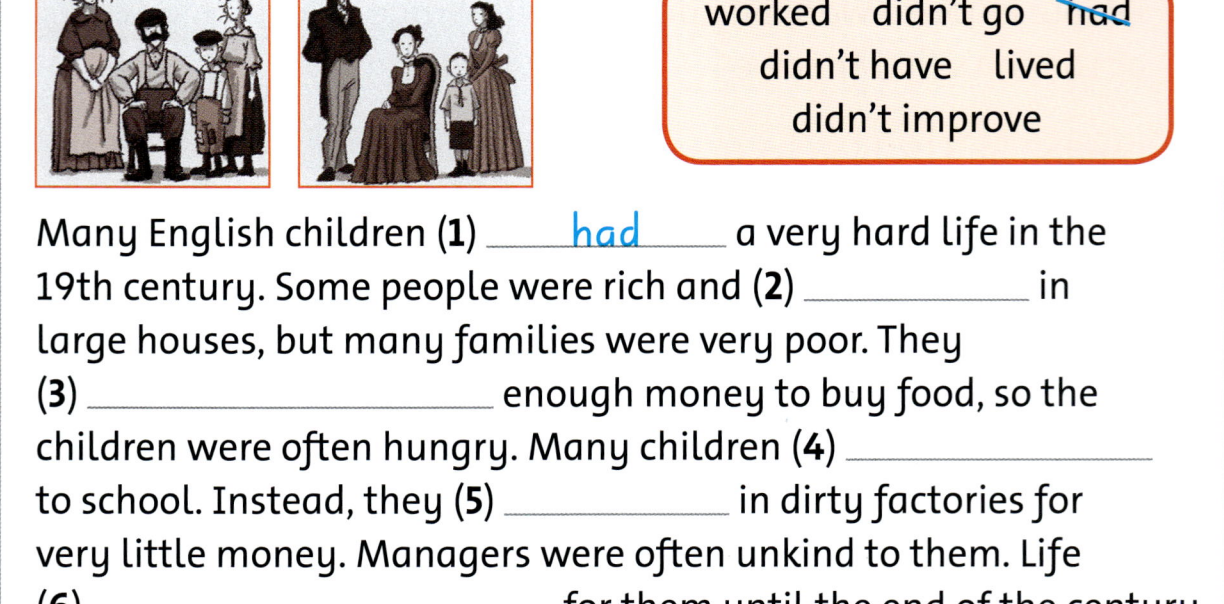

worked   didn't go   ~~had~~
didn't have   lived
didn't improve

Many English children **(1)** _____had_____ a very hard life in the 19th century. Some people were rich and **(2)** _____ in large houses, but many families were very poor. They **(3)** _____ enough money to buy food, so the children were often hungry. Many children **(4)** _____ to school. Instead, they **(5)** _____ in dirty factories for very little money. Managers were often unkind to them. Life **(6)** _____ for them until the end of the century.

2 **Make six sentences about George and Katy in the 19th century.**

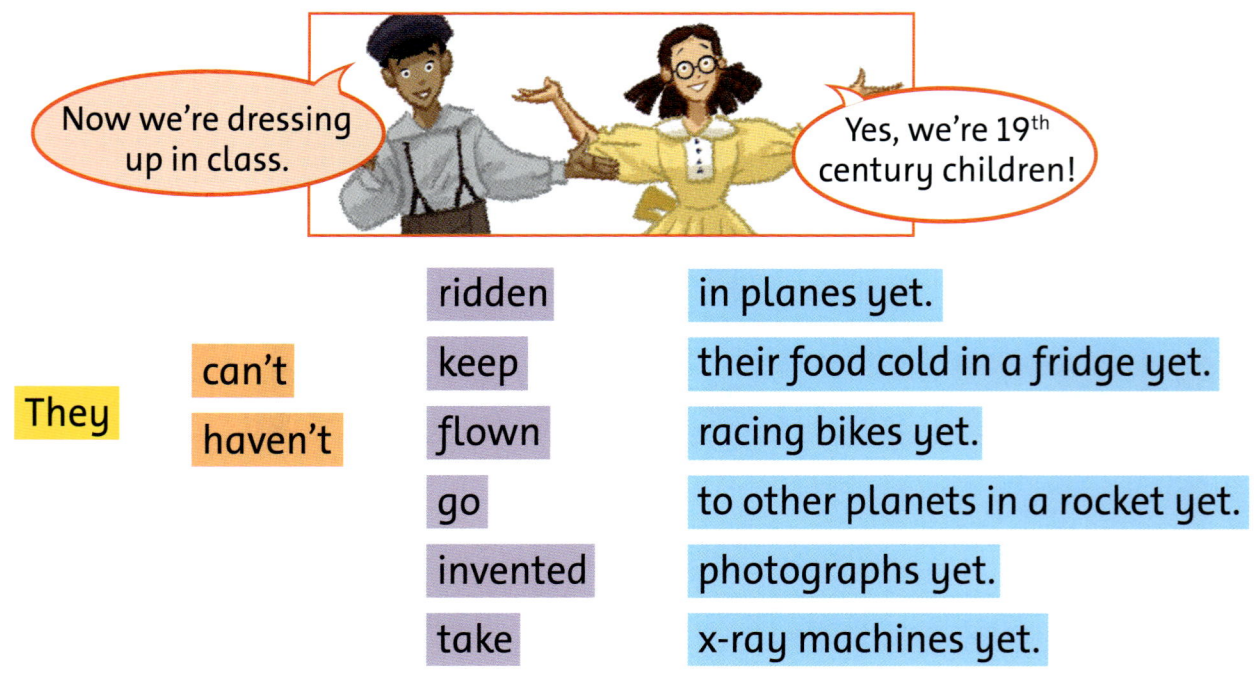

Now we're dressing up in class.

Yes, we're 19th century children!

They	can't	ridden	in planes yet.
	haven't	keep	their food cold in a fridge yet.
		flown	racing bikes yet.
		go	to other planets in a rocket yet.
		invented	photographs yet.
		take	x-ray machines yet.

Reading & listening

1 **Read the conversation and write the words.**

> see   live   ~~visit~~   fly   learn   invent

Teacher: What will life be like in the future?

Holly and Harry: We don't know!

Teacher: Have a guess!

Holly: I hope we'll fly in spaceships and (**1**) _visit_ other planets.

Harry: We might (**2**) _____ round them in our rockets.

George: Perhaps we'll (**3**) _____ on another planet one day.

Katy: We might (**4**) _____ some aliens there!

George: Yes, and we might (**5**) _____ their language!

Katy: Or someone might (**6**) _____ a car with no wheels or tyres, but with wings instead so it can fly.

Today is Friday. We're having our first science lesson. It's about space and the planets!

2 **Listen to the teacher talking about the planets. Write down the information.** 🔊41

Saturn

Number of moons: _____18_____
First rocket round planet: _____ July _____
Name of rocket: _____
Rings round Saturn are very _____.
They are made mostly of water and _____.

Mercury

Number of moons: ___no moons___
First rocket round planet: _____ March _____
Temperature away from sun: _____ zero
Temperature can be: _____ °C
Temperature when sun is out: _____ °C

Listening & speaking

1 Do the speaking activity. **P** 142

> How many moons does Jupiter have?

> It has sixty moons.

2 The children are talking about what they'll do in the future. Listen and draw lines. 🔊 42

Holly

Harry

George

Katy

Sarah

Emma

Robert

3 Have a conversation with your friends about what you'll do in the future.

Flyers practice test

Listen and draw lines. There is one example. 🔊43

Richard   Oliver   Frank   Betty

Michael   Sophia   Lily

Look at the picture and read the story. Write some words to complete the sentences about the story. You can use 1, 2, 3 or 4 words

My first day at school

Hello. My name's George. Last Monday I looked at my calendar. It was the 8th September and that was the day I started my new school. I got up and put on my new uniform. It felt strange. I put my special toy dinosaur in my pocket because it's my lucky toy! Mum gave me some cereal for breakfast but I couldn't eat it because I was excited, but also a bit worried. When I said 'goodbye' to my Mum, she gave me some pieces of chocolate for later. Then I started to walk to school. It was a long way. When I arrived at my new school, I stopped for a minute. Then, I decided I had to be brave, so I walked through the school gates. I was very early. It was only half past eight, but Harry was already in the playground and he was waiting for me. When I saw him, I felt a lot better.

We went into the classroom together and sat down at some desks. They were at the front of the classroom. Next the teacher came in. He was very friendly and told us how to do well at our new school. Then, he took us on a tour of the school. It's a very large school!

After that we had lessons, and at about midday we stopped to eat our lunch in the school restaurant. We had pizza with olives on it – my favourite! Then, after lunch, we went into the playground again. Some other boys in the playground had a football, and they were kicking it and having fun. Harry and I put our trainers on, then went over to them and asked if we could play too. Soon, other boys joined the game and we had two football teams. With my lucky dinosaur still in my pocket I scored two goals, and suddenly I was very popular with all the boys on my team! I was really happy about that. When I went back to class in the afternoon, I already had lots of new friends. Soon the first week of school will be over. I think I'll like it here!

Flyers practice test

Examples

After George got up, he _____put on_____ his new uniform.

George put a toy dinosaur _in his pocket_ to bring him good luck.

Questions

1 On his first day at school, George felt excited but _____ too.

2 George had to walk a _____ to get to his new school.

3 When George walked through the school gates he could see that Harry _____ for him.

4 George and Harry sat down _____ of the classroom.

5 Before they had their lessons, the teacher gave the children _____ the building.

6 At lunch time George ate _____ .

7 All the boys were happy with George because he _____ in the football match.

Revision 3

1 Look at the pictures in the first grid. Write the first letter of each word in the second grid to complete the crossword.

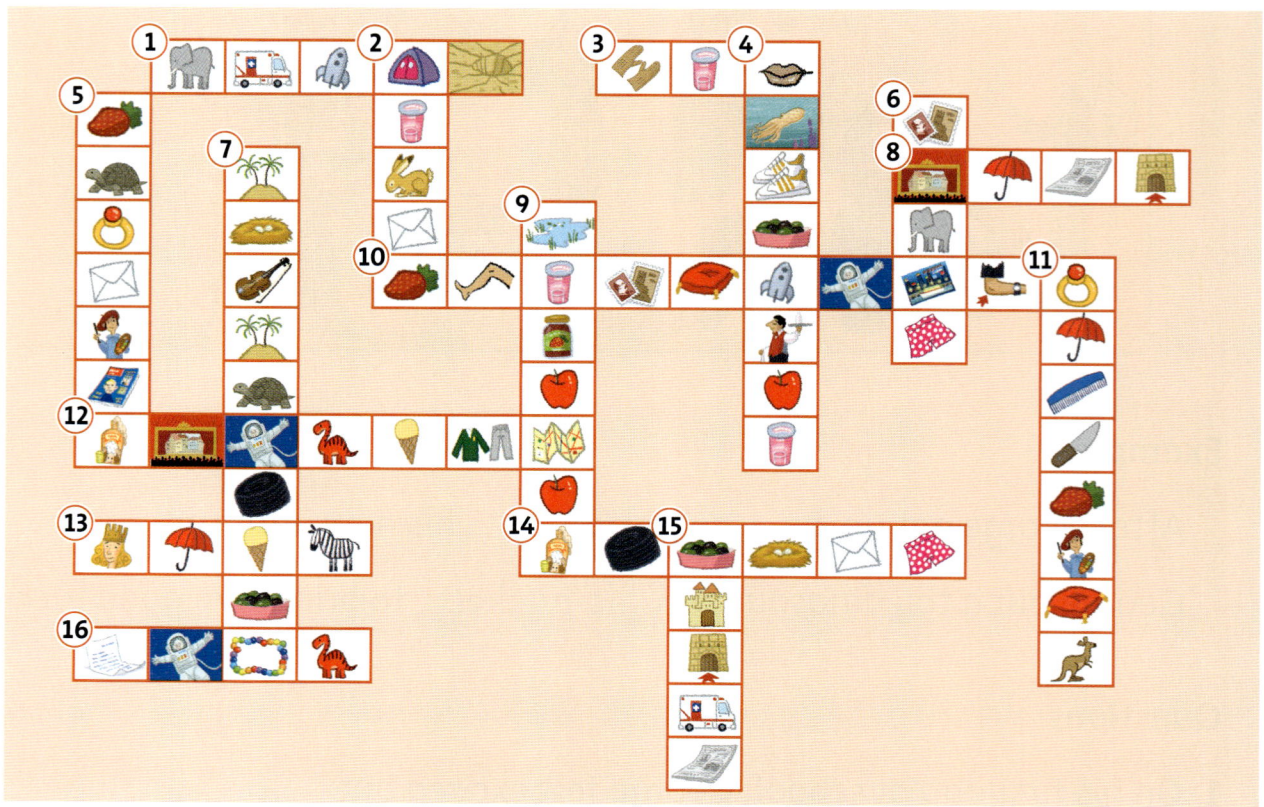

2 Draw lines and make sentences.

1 If there's a rainbow in the sky

2 If it's sunny

3 If it's very windy

4 If it snows

5 If it rains

6 If there's ice on the pond in the garden

7 If there's a storm in the night

I ride down the hills on my sledge.

I take an umbrella with me.

I go fishing in a stream near my house.

I hide under my blanket because it's frightening.

I try to take a picture of it.

I take my kite to the top of a hill and fly it.

I go skating with my friend there.

3 Look at these pictures. They tell a story but they are not in the correct order. With your friend, number the pictures and tell the story.

a

b

c

d

e

f

g

h

i

4 Listen and check. Was your story different? Talk to your friend about all the things that were different in your story. 🔊44

5 **Write the missing words.**

living   believe   go   happened
are   ~~been~~   find   rain
was   fell   is   looked

The Great Ice Age

There have (**1**) _____been_____ about eleven different ice ages.
The last ice age (**2**) _____ called 'The Great Ice Age'. It
(**3**) _____ eleven thousand years ago. During the Great Ice
Age it didn't (**4**) _____. The temperature was too cold for
that, but soft snow (**5**) _____ all over the planet. Before
the ice age, some strange furry animals were (**6**) _____
on our planet. Some were called Woolly Mammoths. They
(**7**) _____ a bit like elephants. Others were called
Cave bears. These were like the bears we can (**8**) _____
to see in zoos today, but they were much bigger. Sadly, these
amazing animals (**9**) _____ now extinct. People
(**10**) _____ they died because they couldn't
(**11**) _____ enough food to eat.

6 **Draw lines to match the questions and answers. Then act.**

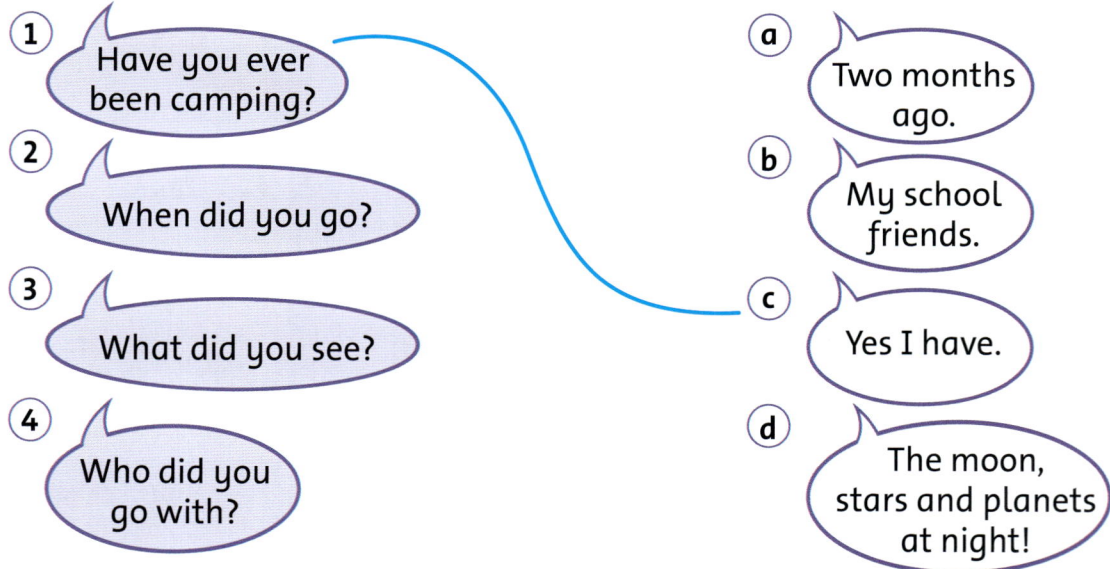

① Have you ever been camping?
② When did you go?
③ What did you see?
④ Who did you go with?

ⓐ Two months ago.
ⓑ My school friends.
ⓒ Yes I have.
ⓓ The moon, stars and planets at night!

7 **Now you ask questions about the pictures below and answer them.**

①  ridden

② 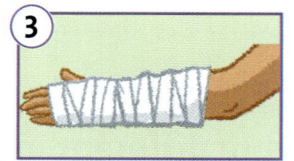 grown

③ broken

④  won

REVISION 3
WORDS   page 117

1 **Look at the pictures and the example. Now you tell the story with a friend.**

It's a very foggy day in winter. Jenny is playing with her dog in the woods behind her house. She's throwing pieces of wood and her dog is catching them.

2 **Write the different times of year under the pictures.**

spring   summer   autumn   winter

_____   _____   _____   _____

3 **Talk about the things you do at different times of year.**

What do you do in ...

 spring?    summer?   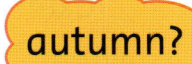 autumn?    winter?

4 **Now do the Speaking test.** P 126

Wordlist

Names

Girls: Betty, Emma, Helen, Holly, Katy, Sarah, Sophia

Boys: David, Frank, George, Harry, Michael, Oliver, Richard, Robert, William

Hello!

April _____

August _____

aunt _____

brother _____

cousin _____

dad _____

December _____

family tree _____

February _____

grandma _____

grandpa _____

husband _____

January _____

July _____

June _____

March _____

May _____

month _____

mum _____

November _____

October _____

September _____

sister _____

surname _____

thousand _____

twins _____

uncle _____

way _____

wife _____

① Our home

after _____

anyone _____

anything _____

anywhere _____

arrive _____

away _____

before _____

bin _____

bit _____

bored _____

borrow _____

broken _____

brush _____

channel _____

chat _____

chess _____

college _____

comb _____

cooker _____

cushion _____

cycle _____

dear _____

diary _____

drums _____

empty _____

envelope _____

everyone _____

everything _____

everywhere _____

file _____

fridge _____

friendly _____

full _____

fun _____

go out _____

important _____

interesting _____

keep _____

key _____

kind _____

late _____

letter _____

little _____

lucky _____

meal _____

much _____

necklace _____

news _____

noisy _____

no-one _____

of course _____

oven _____

paper _____

popular _____

post _____

postcard _____

programme _____

quiet _____

rucksack _____

search _____

shampoo _____

shelf _____

soap _____

somewhere _____

stamps _____

take _____

teach _____

tidy _____

time _____

toothpaste _____

unfriendly _____

unhappy _____

unkind _____

untidy _____

usually _____

violin _____

warm _____

wheel _____

wifi _____

② Going to town

across _____

airport _____

ambulance _____

bank _____

bicycle _____

bridge _____

castle _____

chemist's _____

corner _____

expensive _____

factory _____

fetch _____

fire engine _____

fire station _____

forget _____

front _____

get to _____

hill _____

hotel _____

How long _____

later _____

left _____

middle _____

money _____

motorway _____

museum _____

next _____

other _____

over _____

past _____

police station _____

post office _____

pyjamas _____

railway station _____

remember _____

restaurant _____

right _____

shorts _____

sky _____

skyscraper _____

stadium _____

taxi _____

through _____

traffic _____

university _____

will _____

wood _____

③ Eating out

amazing _____

biscuit _____

bracelet _____

butter _____

chopsticks _____

dangerous _____

delicious _____

excited _____

feel _____

finish _____

flour _____

fork _____

frightened _____

group _____

hard _____

hear _____

honey _____

ill _____

jam _____

knife _____

look like _____

lovely _____

medicine _____

mind _____

olives _____

pepper _____

piece _____

pizza _____

salt _____

smell _____

soft _____

sound _____

spend _____

spoon _____

strawberry _____

sugar _____

surprise _____

tastes _____

tortoise _____

visit _____

wool _____

yoghurt _____

4 At school

a.m. _____

actually _____

agree _____

art _____

beetle _____

card _____

club _____

cut _____

dictionary _____

disappear _____

during _____

enormous _____

excellent _____

geography _____

half _____

history _____

improve _____

information _____

invitation _____

IT _____

join _____

language _____

maths _____

metal _____

midday _____

midnight _____

music _____

o'clock _____

p.m. _____

plastic _____

platform _____

program _____

quarter _____

repeat _____

same _____

save _____

science _____

study _____

subject _____

sure _____

timetable _____

quiz _____

Revision 1

believe _____

minute _____

mix _____

turn on _____

until _____

without _____

5 A day out

act _____

actor _____

ago _____

air _____

also _____

brave _____

cage _____

cartoon _____

cereal _____

cheap _____

cinema _____

circus _____

clown _____

dinosaurs _____

extinct _____

find out _____

frightening _____

gym _____

hate _____

high _____

hole _____

hour _____

million _____

museum _____

ocean _____

pleased _____

project _____

pyramids _____

screen _____

seat _____

sell _____

several _____

special _____

stage _____

stay _____

swing _____

telephone _____

theatre _____

tomorrow _____

tune _____

wild _____

zoo _____

6 Dream jobs

artist _____

astronaut _____

bandage _____

begin _____

businessman/
  woman _____

cook _____

dentist _____

designer _____

doctor _____

each _____

early _____

engineer _____

fast _____

fire fighter _____

happen _____

job _____

journalist _____

lazy _____

look after _____

manager _____

mechanic _____

meeting _____

nowhere _____

nurse _____

office _____

perhaps _____

photographer _____

pilot _____

police officer _____

poor _____

rich _____

singer _____

teacher _____

tennis player _____

waiter _____

7 At the castle

appear _____

bridge _____

building _____

butterfly _____

century _____

conversation _____

costume _____

creature _____

crown _____

date _____

design _____

east _____

entrance _____

exit _____

festival _____

finger _____

flag _____

follow _____

gate _____

glass _____

gold _____

insect _____

interested _____

journey _____

king _____

leave _____

make sure _____

might _____

north _____

postcard _____

queen _____

ring _____

send _____

silver _____

south _____

steps _____

still _____

swan _____

swing _____

touch _____

tour _____

unusual _____

view _____

west _____

wild _____

wonderful _____

8 Sports day!

already _____

competition _____

end _____

explain _____

fall over _____

goal _____

golf _____

just _____

knee _____

match _____

prize _____

race _____

score _____

snack _____

sore _____

team _____

volleyball _____

winner _____

yet _____

Revision 2

engine _____

invent _____

racing car _____

repair _____

suddenly _____

win _____

9 Our camping adventure

alone _____

belt _____

biscuits _____

burn _____

camp _____

cave _____

dark _____

decide _____

deep _____

Earth _____

elbow _____

explore _____

fire _____

fur _____

furry _____

heavy _____

hill _____

horrible _____

kilometre _____

large _____

magazine _____

missing _____

nest _____

newspaper _____

path _____

pocket _____

rock _____

soft _____

stars _____

stone _____

strange _____

tent _____

together _____

torch _____

tyre _____

umbrella _____

whisper _____

whistle _____

wing _____

wood _____

⑩ A good year!

autumn _____

collect _____

enter _____

grow _____

leaf _____

lie _____

pull _____

push _____

sledge _____

snowball _____

snowboard _____

snowman _____

spring _____

summer _____

trip _____

winter _____

wish _____

x-ray _____

⑪ Our summer holidays

camel _____

desert _____

environment _____

ever _____

foggy _____

gloves _____

lift _____

London _____

meet _____

octopus _____

pop music _____

raining _____

rock music _____

should _____

snowing _____

spotted _____

storm _____

striped _____

suitcase _____

sunglasses _____

sunny _____

toe _____

trainers _____

⑫ Past and future

calendar _____

eagle _____

enough _____

future _____

guess _____

hope _____

land _____

past _____

planet _____

pond _____

racing bike _____

ready _____

rocket _____

ski _____

space _____

spaceship _____

steam _____

worried _____

Revision 3

ice _____

Grammar

After and *Before* clauses

after	*After lunch I had my music lesson.*
before	*You put stamps on a letter **before** you post it.*

Where clauses

Here's a map of the town **where** we live.

could

I **could visit** the museum.
She **could buy** soap at the chemist's.
They **could go** to the playground.

will

Will you fetch the key for me, please?
I won't go to town because it's raining.

be, look, sound, feel, taste, smell like

What**'s** your new house **like**?
That **smells like** pizza cooking.
That **sounds like** your telephone ringing
George **looks like** his brother.
This table **feels like** wood, but it's plastic.
This **tastes like** banana ice cream.

make somebody / something + adjective

*That smell **makes me hungry**!*

shall

Shall we go to the cinema this afternoon?
What **shall** we have for dinner?

What time ...?

What time does art club start?
What time is morning break?

made of

The chopsticks **are made of** wood.
The fork **is made of** metal.
What **is** the scarf **made of**?

as ... as ...

An elephant isn't **as** big **as** a dinosaur.
Is that bracelet **as** expensive **as** the necklace?
Do that **as** quickly **as** you can!

be going to

I'm **going to go** to Egypt.	I'm **not going to eat** octopus.
He's **going to go** on an aeroplane.	He **isn't going to go** to the beach.
What **are you going to do** next week?	**Is he going to walk** to school?
I'm **going to ride** my bike every day.	No, **he isn't.**

Tag questions

*She can run fast, **can't she?***
*They play football very well, **don't they?***
*It isn't very warm today, **is it?***
*You aren't going to be late, **are you?***

yet

The children haven't had their snack **yet**.
The competition hasn't started **yet**.

Present perfect

I**'ve** already **had** my lunch.
You **haven't done** your homework yet.
She**'s been** to the cinema this week.
We **haven't finished** reading the book.

Past continuous

I was feeling happy.
The sun was shining brightly.
The teacher was explaining the homework.
The children were walking to school.

while

While Harry was walking through the woods, he hurt his foot.

If clauses

If it's cold, I put on a coat.
If there's a storm, she's frightened.
If it's sunny, they go to the beach.
What do you do **if** it's foggy?

might

You **might** need your coat today.
We **might** go to the beach tomorrow.

should

You **should** take your books on holiday.
We **should** wear sunglasses today.
You **shouldn't** put all your money in your rucksack.
Should we take our hats and gloves when we go skiing?

Irregular verb list

Infinitive	Past simple	Past participle	Infinitive	Past simple	Past participle
be	was/were	been	leave	left	left
begin	began	begun	let	let	let
break	broke	broken	lie	lied	lied
bring	brought	brought	lose/looz/	lost	lost
build	built	built	make	made	made
buy	bought	bought	mean	meant	meant
can	could	—	meet	met	met
catch	caught	caught	put	put	put
choose	chose	chosen	read	read/red/	read/red/
come	came	come	ride	rode	ridden
cut	cut	cut	run	ran	ran
do	did	done	say	said/sed/	said/sed/
draw	drew	drawn	see	saw	seen
drink	drank	drunk	sell	sold	sold
drive	drove	driven	send	sent	sent
dry	dried	dried	sing	sang	sung
eat	ate	eaten	sit	sat	sat
fall	fell	fallen	sleep	slept	slept
feed	fed	fed	smell	smelt	smelt
feel	felt	felt	speak	spoke	spoken
find	found	found	spell	spelled/spelt	spelled/spelt
fly	flew	flown	spend	spent	spent
forget	forgot	forgotten	stand	stood	stood
get	got	gotten	steal	stole	stolen
give	gave	given	swim	swam	swum
go	went	gone	swing	swung	swung
grow	grew	grown	take	took	taken
have	had	had	teach	taught	taught
have got	had got	have gotten	tell	told	told
hear	heard	heard	think	thought	thought
hide	hid	hidden	throw	threw	thrown
hit	hit	hit	understand	understood	understood
hold	held	held	wake up	woke up	woken up
hurt	hurt	hurt	wear	wore	worn
keep	kept	kept	win	won	won
know	knew	known	write	wrote	written
learn	learned/learnt	learned/learnt			